Georgia Grade 8 Mathematics 52 Days of CRCT Preparation

Supporting the Georgia Performance Standards

STUDENT EDITION

The Georgia Mathematics Test Preparation book helps students prepare for the Criterion-Referenced Competency Tests (CRCT). The Support Book begins with a list of the Georgia Performance Standards to help the teachers easily review the core content of the standards. The Support Book contains information on "Tips for Taking Multiple Choice Tests" that provides useful test taking strategies to help students be successful on the CRCT. Additionally, there is a Diagnostic Test for teachers to use to assess what the students know and what they need to practice. Following the Diagnostic Test, this book contains practice sheets for each Georgia Performance Standard using the state format of multiple choice. A Georgia CRCT Practice Test is included along with a Diagnostic Scoring Sheet and the answers. For a complete overview of the Support Book contents, see pages ix–xi.

D1456035

McDougal Littell

A DIVISION OF HOUGHTON MIFFLIN COMPANY

Contents

How To Use This Book

Using the Georgia Mathematics—Course 3
52 Days of CRCT Preparation
Supporting the Georgia Performance Standards

Georgia Performance Standards   The Georgia Performance Standards are listed in this book as a quick reference for teachers to see how the Georgia Performance Standards provide clear expectations for assessment, instruction, and student work. The performance standards isolate and identify the skills needed to be successful at problem solving, reasoning, communicating, and making connections with other information. Performance standards also guide the teacher on how to assess the extent to which the student knows the material or how they are able to manipulate and apply them to the content.

Tips for Taking Multiple Choice Tests   This section of the book summarizes test- taking tips for students and provides strategies for choosing correct answers on multiple choice tests. Teachers can use these pages to work with students to help them feel confident in their test-taking abilities leading to self-assurance and ultimate success. These pages should be referred to both before and after the diagnostic test as well as the practice test. Additionally, students can incorporate the strategies as they work through the practice sheets.

Diagnostic Test   This test is offered as a tool for teachers to use to determine their students knowledge of the core content of the Georgia Performance Standards. By utilizing this test, teachers will be able to determine which standards need additional focus to help the students be successful on the CRCT.

Georgia Performance Standards Practice   The practice section of this book provides multiple choice questions for the benchmarks of the Georgia Performance Standards for 52 days. The practice sheets allow the teacher to easily focus on each individual benchmark helping the students reach mastery. Teachers can assign these pages one day at a time or focus on particular pages based on the results of the diagnostic test.

Georgia CRCT Practice Test   A standardized practice test is provided that is designed in a style that is similar to the CRCT. At the end of the 52 days, teachers can administer this test as a follow up to the work done in preparation for the test. The results of the test can be recorded using the **Diagnostic Scoring Sheets.** The scoring sheets provide a tally box for you to record the number of items associated with each Georgia Performance Standard that the student answered correctly. If you wish, these scoring sheets may be given to students for self-assessment. Students can use the tally box to note their correct answers and see if they need to work additionally on certain standards.

Georgia Performance Standards

NUMBER AND OPERATIONS
Students will understand the numeric and geometric meaning of square root, apply properties of integer exponents, and use scientific notation.

M8N1
Students will understand different representations of numbers including square roots, exponents, and scientific notation.

M8N1.a
Find square roots of perfect squares.

M8N1.b
Recognize the (positive) square root of a number as a length of a side of a square with a given area.

M8N1.c
Recognize square roots as points and as lengths on a number line.

M8N1.d
Understand that the square root of 0 is 0 and that every positive number has two square roots that are opposite in sign.

M8N1.e
Recognize and use the radical symbol to denote the positive square root of a positive number.

M8N1.f
Estimate square roots of positive numbers.

M8N1.g
Simplify, add, subtract, multiply, and divide expressions containing square roots.

M8N1.h
Distinguish between rational and irrational numbers.

M8N1.i
Simplify expressions containing integer exponents.

M8N1.j
Express and use numbers in scientific notation.

M8N1.k
Use appropriate technologies to solve problems involving square roots, exponents, and scientific notation.

GEOMETRY
Students will use and apply geometric properties of plane figures, including congruence and the Pythagorean theorem.

M8G1
Students will understand and apply the properties of parallel and perpendicular lines and understand the meaning of congruence.

M8G1.a
Investigate characteristics of parallel and perpendicular lines both algebraically and geometrically.

M8G1.b
Apply properties of angle pairs formed by parallel lines cut by a transversal.

M8G1.c
Understand the properties of the ratio of segments of parallel lines cut by one or more transversals.

M8G1.d
Understand the meaning of congruence: that all corresponding angles are congruent and all corresponding sides are congruent.

M8G2
Students will understand and use the Pythagorean Theorem.

M8G2.a
Apply properties of right triangles, including the Pythagorean Theorem.

M8G2.b
Recognize and interpret the Pythagorean Theorem as a statement about areas of squares on the sides of a right triangle.

ALGEBRA Students will use linear algebra to represent, analyze and solve problems. They will use equations, tables, and graphs to investigate linear relations and functions, paying particular attention to slope as a rate of change.

M8A1
Students will use algebra to represent, analyze, and solve problems.

M8A1.a
Represent a given situation using algebraic expressions or equations in one variable.

M8A1.b
Simplify and evaluate algebraic expressions.

M8A1.c
Solve algebraic equations in one variable, including equations involving absolute values.

M8A1.d
Interpret solutions in problem contexts.

M8A2
Students will understand and graph inequalities in one variable.

M8A2.a
Represent a given situation using an inequality in one variable.

M8A2.b
Use the properties of inequality to solve inequalities.

M8A2.c
Graph the solution of an inequality on a number line.

M8A2.d
Interpret solutions in problem contexts.

Georgia Performance Standards *(continued)*

M8A3 Students will understand relations and linear functions.
M8A3.a Recognize a relation as a correspondence between varying quantities.
M8A3.b Recognize a function as a correspondence between inputs and outputs where the output for each input must be unique.
M8A3.c Distinguish between relations that are functions and those that are not functions.
M8A3.d Recognize functions in a variety of representations and a variety of contexts.
M8A3.e Use tables to describe sequences recursively and with a formula in closed form.
M8A3.f Understand and recognize arithmetic sequences as linear functions with whole number input values.
M8A3.g Interpret the constant difference in an arithmetic sequence as the slope of the associated linear function.
M8A3.h Identify relations and functions as linear or nonlinear.
M8A3.i Translate among verbal, tabular, graphic, and algebraic representations of functions.
M8A4 Students will graph and analyze graphs of linear equations.
M8A4.a Interpret slope as a rate of change.
M8A4.b Determine the meaning of the slope and y-intercept in a given situation.
M8A4.c Graph equations of the form $y = mx + b$.
M8A4.d Graph equations of the form $ax + by = c$.
M8A4.e Determine the equation of a line given a graph, numerical information that defines the line, or a context involving a linear relationship.
M8A4.f Solve problems involving linear relationships.
M8A5 Students will understand systems of linear equations and use them to solve problems.

M8A5.a
Given a problem context, write an appropriate system of linear equations.

M8A5.b
Solve systems of equations graphically and algebraically, using technology as appropriate.

M8A5.c
Interpret solutions in problem contexts.

DATA ANALYSIS AND PROBABILITY
Students will use and understand set theory and simple counting techniques; determine the theoretical probability of simple events; and make inferences from data, particularly data that can be modeled by linear functions.

M8D1
Students will apply basic concepts of set theory.

M8D1.a
Demonstrate relationships among sets through use of Venn Diagrams.

M8D1.b
Determine subsets, complements, intersection, and union of sets.

M8D1.c
Use set notation to denote elements of a set.

M8D2
Students will determine the number of outcomes related to a given event.

M8D2.a
Use tree diagrams to find the number of outcomes.

M8D2.b
Apply addition and multiplication counting principles.

M8D3
Students will use the basic laws of probability.

M8D3.a
Find the probability of simple, independent events.

M8D3.b
Find the probability of compound, independent events.

M8D4
Students will organize, interpret, and make inferences from statistical data.

M8D4.a
Gather data that can be modeled with a linear function.

M8D4.b
Estimate and determine a line of best fit from a scatter plot.

Tips for Taking Multiple Choice Tests

To do your best on a multiple choice test, you need to work steadily and efficiently. The following ideas will help you keep on track as you work through a test successfully and with confidence.

Read questions carefully. Before you begin to answer a question, read it completely. Key information may come at the end of the question. Reread the question if you are not sure you understand what it is asking.

Don't read the answers too soon. Whenever possible, answer the question before looking at the answer choices. Even if you cannot come up with the answer right away, your first try may help you understand the question better and eliminate some answers.

Read all choices before marking your answer. Be sure you know all of your options before choosing an answer. If you are having difficulty understanding a question, the answer choices may help you understand what the question is asking.

Pace yourself. Don't try to go through the test as quickly as you can—this can lead to careless mistakes. Work steadily.

Don't get distracted. Resist the temptation to look up every time you hear a rustling of paper or a scooting desk. Focus on *your* paper and *your* thought process.

Don't look for patterns. Especially on standardized tests, there is no way to tell what answer comes next by looking at previous answers. Don't waste precious time looking for a pattern that isn't there.

Mark your answer sheet carefully. Take a moment to make sure you mark your answer in the correct place. This is especially important if you skip one or more problems. When answering multiple choice tests, be sure to fill in the bubble completely and, if you change an answer, to erase all traces of your old mark.

Check your answers. If you have time, go back and check your answers, filling in answers to any problems you may have skipped. *However . . .*

Be SURE before you change an answer. Your first answer is usually your best answer. Don't change an answer unless you are certain the original answer is incorrect.

If you get stuck, it is important to stay relaxed and confident even if you struggle with some problems.

Stay calm. Realize that this is only a small part of the test. Don't let a momentary obstacle affect your confidence.

Don't spend too much time on one problem. If you find a problem especially difficult, move on to others that are easier for you. Make the best guess you can go on, or skip the problem entirely and return to it later if time permits.

Make an educated guess. If you know some of the choices are wrong, eliminate those and make the best guess you can from the rest.

Tips for Taking Multiple Choice Tests (continued)

If opposite answers are given as choices, one of them is usually the right answer.

Work backward. If you are having a difficult time with a problem, you may be able to substitute the answers into the problem and see which one is correct.

MULTIPLE CHOICE QUESTIONS

If you have difficulty solving a multiple choice problem directly, you can try another approach. You may want to eliminate incorrect answer choices to obtain the correct answer.

PROBLEM 1

A helideck is a takeoff and landing area for helicopters on ships. A rectangular helideck has a length of 16.76 meters and a width of 12.19 meters. What is the best estimate for the perimeter of the helideck?

A 29 meters **B** 58 meters **C** 80 meters **D** 204 meters

METHOD 1

SOLVE DIRECTLY Round the length and width of the helideck to the nearest whole number. Then use the perimeter formula.

STEP 1 **Identify** the length ℓ and width w.
$\ell = 16.76$ m $w = 12.19$ m

STEP 2 **Round** the length and width to the nearest whole number.
16.76 m $\longrightarrow$ 17 m
12.19 m $\longrightarrow$ 12 m

STEP 3 **Write** the formula for perimeter. Substitute 17 for ℓ and 12 for w.

$$
\begin{aligned}
\text{Perimeter} &= 2\ell + 2w \\
&= 2(17) + 2(12) \\
&= 34 + 24 \\
&= 58
\end{aligned}
$$

The correct answer is B.

METHOD 2

ELIMINATE CHOICES In some cases, you can identify choices of a multiple choice question that can be eliminated.

STEP 1 **Make** a low estimate. Two sides of the helideck have a length of about 17 meters. So, because $17 + 17 = 34$, you can eliminate choice A.

STEP 2 **Make** a high estimate. The length and width of the helideck are both less than 20 meters. So, because $4 \times 20 = 80$, you can eliminate choices C and D. These perimeters are too long.

The correct answer is B.

Tips for Taking Multiple Choice Tests (continued)

PROBLEM 2

The data set shows the altitudes, in miles, of seven airplanes. How far above the median altitude is an eighth airplane that has an altitude of 7.12 miles?

6.51, 6.63, 6.53, 7.01, 6.61, 6.82, 6.42

A 0.11   **B** 0.51   **C** 0.7   **D** 1.1

METHOD 1

SOLVE DIRECTLY Find the median. Then find the difference between the median and the altitude.

STEP 1   **Write** the altitudes from least to greatest.

6.42, 6.51, 6.53, 6.61, 6.63, 6.82, 7.01

STEP 2   The middle number is 6.61, so the median is 6.61.

STEP 3   **Find** the difference between the median altitude and the altitude of the eighth airplane.

$$\begin{array}{r} 7.12 \\ -\ 6.61 \\ \hline 0.51 \end{array}$$

The correct answer is B.

METHOD 2

ELIMINATE CHOICES In some cases, you can identify choices of a multiple choice question that can be eliminated.

The value 0.11 represents the difference in altitude between the highest altitude, 7.01 miles, and 7.12 miles. The difference must be greater than this for the mean altitude, so you can eliminate choice A.

The value 0.7 represents the difference in altitude between the lowest altitude, 6.42 miles, and 7.12 miles. The difference must be less than this for the median altitude, so you can eliminate choice C.

None of the other airplanes are more than a mile in altitude than the eighth plane at its altitude of 7.12 miles, so you can eliminate choice D.

The correct answer is B.

Georgia Diagnostic Test

1. What is the square root $\sqrt{144}$?

Ⓐ 0.12

Ⓑ 12

Ⓒ 14

Ⓓ 144

2. What is the square root $-\sqrt{529}$?

Ⓐ 529

Ⓑ 230

Ⓒ 23

Ⓓ 2.3

3. What is the side length of a square having the given area?

$$A = 289 \text{ m}^2$$

Ⓐ 4.25 m

Ⓑ 8.5 m

Ⓒ 17 m

Ⓓ 34 m

4. What is the length of one side of a square garden that has an area of 625 square feet?

Ⓐ 23 ft.

Ⓑ 25 ft.

Ⓒ 35 ft.

Ⓓ 65 ft.

5. Match the point on the line with the correct number below.

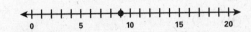

Ⓐ $\sqrt{9}$

Ⓑ $\sqrt{27}$

Ⓒ $\sqrt{72}$

Ⓓ $\sqrt{81}$

6. Match the point on the line with the correct number below.

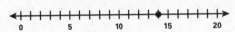

Ⓐ $\sqrt{14}$

Ⓑ $\sqrt{168}$

Ⓒ $\sqrt{196}$

Ⓓ $\sqrt{225}$

7. What are the two square roots of 6.25?

Ⓐ ±0.25

Ⓑ ±3.125

Ⓒ −2.5, 0.25

Ⓓ ±2.5

8. What are the two square roots of the number?

$$160,000$$

Ⓐ −400, 400

Ⓑ −40, 40

Ⓒ −40,000, 40,000

Ⓓ −4000, 4000

Diagnostic Test

Georgia Diagnostic Test

9. What is the value of $\sqrt{36}$?

- (A) 6
- (B) 9
- (C) 18
- (D) 216

10. Evaulate the number $\sqrt{121}$.

- (A) 10.5
- (B) 11
- (C) 11.5
- (D) 13

11. What is the approximate square root to the nearest whole number $\sqrt{74}$?

- (A) 11
- (B) 90
- (C) 8.6
- (D) 9

12. What is the approximate square root to the nearest whole number $\sqrt{46}$?

- (A) 5
- (B) 6
- (C) 7
- (D) 8

13. What is the value of $\sqrt{9} + \sqrt{16}$?

- (A) 25
- (B) 19
- (C) 7
- (D) 5

14. What is the square root $\sqrt{\frac{25}{64}}$?

- (A) $\frac{1}{6}$
- (B) $\frac{5}{8}$
- (C) $\frac{1}{8}$
- (D) $\frac{1}{12}$

15. Which of the following is a rational number?

- (A) $-\sqrt{\frac{1}{11}}$
- (B) $-\sqrt{\frac{1}{81}}$
- (C) $\sqrt{\frac{1}{19}}$
- (D) $\sqrt{\frac{1}{24}}$

16. Which number is irrational?

- (A) $\frac{1}{19}$
- (B) $3.\overline{14285}$
- (C) $-\sqrt{169}$
- (D) $\sqrt{87}$

Georgia Diagnostic Test

17. What is the value of the expression for the given value of a?

$$a^3 \text{ when } a = 6$$

Ⓐ 36

Ⓑ 108

Ⓒ 180

Ⓓ 216

18. What is the value of the expression for the given value of c?

$$c^1 \text{ when } c = 9$$

Ⓐ 0

Ⓑ 1

Ⓒ 9

Ⓓ 10

19. What is 12,003 written in scientific notation?

Ⓐ 1.2003×10^3

Ⓑ 12.003×10^4

Ⓒ 1.2003×10^4

Ⓓ 2.003×10^4

20. What is 0.0057 written in scientific notation?

Ⓐ 1.0057×10^{-3}

Ⓑ 5.7×10^{-3}

Ⓒ 5.7×10^3

Ⓓ 5.7×10^{-4}

21. What is the square root to the nearest tenth? (You may use a calculator.)

$$-\sqrt{0.81}$$

Ⓐ -0.45

Ⓑ -0.045

Ⓒ -0.9

Ⓓ -0.09

22. What is the square root to the nearest tenth? (You may use a calculator.)

$$-\sqrt{31}$$

Ⓐ 5.2

Ⓑ 5.6

Ⓒ 15.5

Ⓓ -15.5

23. Two points, $A(0, 0)$ and $B(8, 6)$ appear on a coordinate plane. What is the slope of the line that passes through them? What is the slope of a line perpendicular to $\overrightarrow{AB}$?

Ⓐ $\dfrac{4}{3}, \dfrac{4}{3}$

Ⓑ $\dfrac{3}{4}, -\dfrac{4}{3}$

Ⓒ $8, \dfrac{1}{8}$

Ⓓ $\dfrac{1}{6}, 6$

Georgia Diagnostic Test

24. Two points, $A(-6, -5)$ and $B(1, 9)$ appear on a coordinate plane. What is the slope of the line that passes through them? What is the slope of a line parallel to $\overrightarrow{AB}$?

   Ⓐ $\frac{1}{2}$, -2

   Ⓑ $\frac{5}{4}$, $-\frac{5}{4}$

   Ⓒ 2, 2

   Ⓓ $\frac{1}{7}$, $-\frac{1}{7}$

25. What is the measure of angle 1?

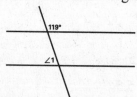

   Ⓐ 119°

   Ⓑ 90°

   Ⓒ 241°

   Ⓓ 61°

26. What is the measure of ∠10?

   Ⓐ 104°

   Ⓑ 135°

   Ⓒ 121°

   Ⓓ 59°

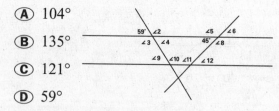

27. If the 3 horizontal lines are parallel, find the value of x.

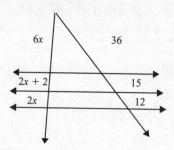

   Ⓐ 1

   Ⓑ 2

   Ⓒ 4

   Ⓓ 6

28. Lines $\overleftrightarrow{UP}$, $\overleftrightarrow{TQ}$, and $\overleftrightarrow{SR}$ are parallel. Which of the following must be true?

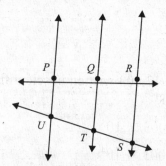

   Ⓐ $\dfrac{PQ}{QR} = \dfrac{UT}{QR}$

   Ⓑ $\dfrac{TS}{UT} = \dfrac{QR}{PQ}$

   Ⓒ $\dfrac{QR}{RS} = \dfrac{TS}{RS}$

   Ⓓ $\dfrac{PQ}{PR} = \dfrac{US}{TS}$

Georgia Diagnostic Test

29. $\triangle OPT$ is congruent to $\triangle IDL$. Which completes the congruence statement?
a. $\angle O \cong$ ____   b. $\overline{OT} \cong$ ____

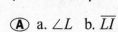

   Ⓐ a. $\angle L$ b. $\overline{LI}$

   Ⓑ a. $\angle L$ b. $\overline{LD}$

   Ⓒ a. $\angle I$ b. $\overline{IL}$

   Ⓓ none of these

30. Given that these triangles are congruent, which completes the congruence statement? a. $\overline{LD} \cong$ ____   b. $\angle I \cong$ ____

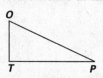

   Ⓐ a. $\overline{PT}$ b. $\angle P$

   Ⓑ a. $\overline{OT}$ b. $\angle O$

   Ⓒ a. $\overline{PO}$ b. $\angle O$

   Ⓓ none of these

31. What is the length of c? Round to the nearest hundredth, if necessary.

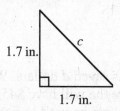

   Ⓐ 2.43 in.

   Ⓑ 2.89 in.

   Ⓒ 3.39 in.

   Ⓓ 3.68 in.

32. Which set of numbers is not a Pythagorean triple?

   Ⓐ 8, 17, 15

   Ⓑ 5, 12, 14

   Ⓒ 15, 20, 25

   Ⓓ 15, 36, 39

33. What is the area of square $ABCD$?

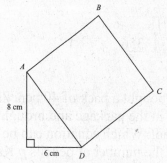

   Ⓐ 64 cm²

   Ⓑ 81 cm²

   Ⓒ 100 cm²

   Ⓓ 144 cm²

34. If the area of square $ABCD$ is 25 in.², what is the area of square $AEFG$?

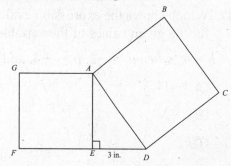

   Ⓐ 9 in.²

   Ⓑ 12.5 in.²

   Ⓒ 16 in.²

   Ⓓ 25.25 in.²

Georgia Diagnostic Test

35. Sharona wants to arrange her stamp collection so that there are 18 stamps on each page. If she has 356 stamps and buys x more stamps at the hobby shop, which expression shows how many display pages she needs?

  (A) $x - \dfrac{356}{18}$

  (B) $\dfrac{x + 18}{356}$

  (C) $\dfrac{x + 356}{18}$

  (D) $18 + \dfrac{356}{x}$

36. Karen bought a pack of 40 pencils. She left 24 in the package and brought some to school. Which equation can be used to find the number of pencils p Karen brought to school?

  (A) $40 + 24 = p$

  (B) $p - 24 = 40$

  (C) $p - 40 = 24$

  (D) $24 + p = 40$

37. Which shows the expression evaluated for the given values of the variables?

  $a - b + c$, when $a = -2$, $b = -4$, and $c = -8$

  (A) -14

  (B) -2

  (C) 2

  (D) -10

38. Which shows the expression evaluated for the given values of the variables?

  $-y - z$, when $y = 40$ and $z = -22$

  (A) -62

  (B) -18

  (C) 18

  (D) 62

39. What is the solution to this equation?

  $$-2(-6)x = -48$$

  (A) -6

  (B) -4

  (C) 4

  (D) 6

40. Which of these expressions is equivalent to the following?

  $$2x + \left| -5 \right| = 13$$

  (A) $x = 4$

  (B) $x = 8$

  (C) $x = 9$

  (D) $x = 18$

41. Terry has saved d dollars. When he saves $23 more, he will have $45. Which equation can be used to find d?

  (A) $d - 23 = 45$

  (B) $d + 45 = 23$

  (C) $23 - d = 45$

  (D) $d + 23 = 45$

42. The outings club can hike at an average rate of 2 miles per hour on good trails. If the drive to the trail head for this Saturday's hike is $1\frac{1}{2}$ hours in each direction, which equation can they use to calculate the distance, m, in miles that they can hike on a $9\frac{1}{2}$ hour outing?

Ⓐ $9\frac{1}{2} = 2m + 3$

Ⓑ $9\frac{1}{2} = \frac{m}{2} + 3$

Ⓒ $9\frac{1}{2} m = 3$

Ⓓ $9\frac{1}{2} = \frac{m + 3}{2}$

43. A DVD player costs $89. You want to buy a player and a DVD with the $110 that you have to spend. Which inequality shows the amount that you can spend, d, on the DVD?

Ⓐ $d \le \$110 - \$89$

Ⓑ $d \ge \$110 - \$89$

Ⓒ $d - \$89 \le \$110$

Ⓓ $d - \$110 \le \$89$

44. Shares of a company's stock cost $13, and there is a $10 service charge for the transaction. Which inequality below could be used to calculate the whole number of shares that could be purchased for $325?

Ⓐ $13s + 10 \ge 325$

Ⓑ $13s + 10 \le 325$

Ⓒ $13s = 325 + 10$

Ⓓ $13s \le 325 + 10$

45. What values of x make this inequality true?

$$-x + 14 \le 22$$

Ⓐ $x \ge 8$

Ⓑ $x \le 8$

Ⓒ $x \ge 36$

Ⓓ $x \le 36$

46. Solve the inequality.

$$\frac{y}{2} - 3 > 9$$

Ⓐ $y > 6$

Ⓑ $y < 24$

Ⓒ $y < 12$

Ⓓ $y > 24$

47. Which inequality is represented by the graph?

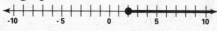

Ⓐ $2m + 7 \le 11$

Ⓑ $m + 7 \ge 11$

Ⓒ $2m + 7 \ge 11$

Ⓓ $m + 7 \le 11$

48. Solve the inequality. Which graph represents its solution?

$$5 - 4m \ge -15$$

Ⓐ
Ⓑ
Ⓒ
Ⓓ

Diagnostic Test

Georgia Diagnostic Test

49. The pep club orders pizza at an evening meeting. Each pizza is cut into 8 slices. Which inequality shows the number of pizzas, p, that must be ordered to be sure that each person gets 2 slices if n people attend the meeting?

A $p \geq 0.25n$

B $p \leq 0.25n$

C $2p \geq 0.25n$

D $2p \leq 0.25n$

50. On a field trip, each bus can carry 40 passengers. Which inequality can be used to calculate the number of buses b needed to take x classes of 25 students?

A $b \geq \dfrac{40}{25x}$

B $b \leq (40)(25x)$

C $b \leq \dfrac{25x}{40}$

D $b \geq \dfrac{25x}{40}$

51. Jeffrey uses 28 nails to build a picture frame. Which completes the table?

Picture frame	1	2	3	4	5
Nails	28	56	84		

A 140, 168

B 112, 140

C 88, 93

D 102, 130

52. There are 16 pastries per carton. Which completes the table?

Carton	1	2	3	4	5
Pastries	16	32	48		

A 80, 96

B 54, 70

C 52, 57

D 64, 80

53. Which table of values represents the function rule $3x + y = 9$?

A

Input x	−2	−1	0	1
Output y	15	12	9	6

B

Input x	−2	−1	0	1
Output y	−15	−12	−9	−6

C

Input x	−2	−1	0	1
Output y	9	9	9	9

D

Input x	−2	−1	0	4
Output y	14	13	8	5

54. Which function rule relates x and y?

Input x	1	2	3	4	5
Output y	0	−7	−14	−21	−28

A $y = -6x + 6$

B $y = 6x - 6$

C $y = -7x + 7$

D $y = 7x + 7$

Georgia Diagnostic Test

55. Which of the following relations cannot be a function?

(A)

Input x	Output y
−6	9
−5	7
−4	5

(B)

Input x	Output y
−5	9
−4	7
−5	5

(C)

Input x	Output y
−3	9
−4	7
−5	5

(D)

Input x	Output y
−3	5
−6	2
−9	5

56. Which line does not represent a function of x?

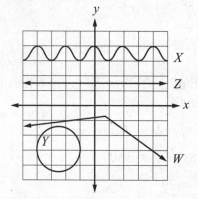

(A) W

(B) X

(C) Y

(D) Z

57. Every member of the drama club sells 15 tickets to the school play. The box office sells another 215 tickets. Which function rule describes the total number of tickets sold if the club has x members.

(A) $t = 15x - 215$

(B) $t = \frac{x}{15} + 215$

(C) $t = \frac{15}{x} + 215$

(D) $t = 15x + 215$

58. Which table of values represents the function rule $-2x + y = 8$

(A)

Input x	1	2	3	4	5
Output y	6	4	2	0	−2

(B)

Input x	1	2	3	4	5
Output y	10	8	6	4	2

(C)

Input x	1	2	3	4	5
Output y	10	12	14	16	18

(D)

Input x	1	2	3	4	5
Output y	10	14	18	22	26

59. Which function rule relates x and y?

Input x	1	2	3	4	5
Output y	1	−2	−5	−8	−11

(A) $y = 3x + 4$

(B) $y = -3x - 4$

(C) $y = -3x + 4$

(D) $y = -x + 4$

Georgia Diagnostic Test

60. Which function rule relates x and y?

Input x	1	2	3	4	5
Output y	15	14	13	12	11

   (A) $y = -x + 16$

   (B) $y = 16x - 1$

   (C) $y = x + 16$

   (D) $y = -x - 16$

61. Which numbers complete the table below if the function is linear?

Teams	1	2	3	4	5
Students	21	42	63		

   (A) 84, 105   **(B)** 67, 72

   (C) 105, 126   **(D)** 25, 29

62. Lynn runs at a rate of 8 miles per hour. Which completes the table?

Hours	1	2	3	4	5
Miles	8	16	24		

   (A) 32, 44   **(B)** 32, 40

   (C) 30, 36   **(D)** 40, 48

63. What is the slope of the line that represents the function in the table below?

x	2	3	4	5
$f(x)$	8	11	14	17

   (A) $\dfrac{1}{2}$

   (B) 2

   (C) 3

   (D) 4

64. What is the slope of the line that represents the function in the table below?

x	-1	0	1	2
$f(x)$	5	3	1	-1

   (A) -2

   (B) -1

   (C) $-\dfrac{1}{2}$

   (D) 2

65. Which of the following is not a linear function?

   (A) $y = -2x - 0.7$

   (B) $18x - y = 350$

   (C) $y = 29$

   (D) $y = (2x)(x) + 43$

Georgia Diagnostic Test

66. Which of the following is not a linear function?

   A $y = -\dfrac{2}{x} + 26$

   D $y = -\dfrac{x}{2} + 26$

   C $y - \dfrac{2x}{9} + 26 = 0$

   C $y - 26 = \dfrac{2x}{9} + 12$

67. Which describes the pattern of the total number of pencils sold for every packages of 8 sold?

$$8,\ 16,\ 24,\ 28,\ \dots$$

   A add eight to find the next term

   B multiply term by eight to find next term

   C add nine and subtract two to find next term

   D multiply term by seven to find next term

68. Which is the graph of the function $y = -4x$?

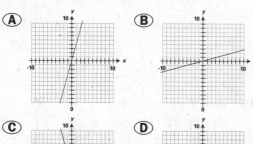
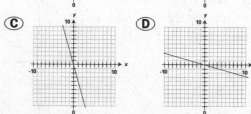

69. The y-axis of the graph represents the length of a balloon in inches. The x-axis represents the time in days passed. Which statement is true?

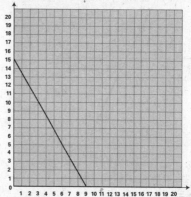

   A The rate at which the size of the balloon decreases gets faster each day.

   B The rate at which the size of the balloon increases remains constant.

   C The rate at which the size of the balloon increases gets slower each day.

   D The rate at which the size of the balloon decreases remains constant.

70. Which shows the slope of the line?

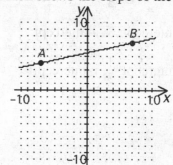

   A $-\dfrac{3}{14}$

   B $-\dfrac{14}{3}$

   C $\dfrac{14}{3}$

   D $\dfrac{3}{14}$

Georgia Diagnostic Test

71. Which shows the equation of the graph in slope-intercept form?

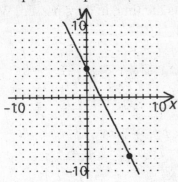

(A) $y = x + 4$

(B) $y = 2x + 4$

(C) $y = -x + 4$

(D) $y = -2x + 4$

72. Which shows the intercepts of the graph of the equation?

$$2y = 4x - 6$$

(A) x-intercept: $\frac{3}{2}$, y-intercept: -3

(B) x-intercept: $\frac{2}{3}$, y-intercept: $\frac{1}{3}$

(C) x-intercept: 3, y-intercept: $\frac{3}{2}$

(D) x-intercept: $\frac{1}{3}$, y-intercept: $\frac{2}{3}$

73. Which shows a graph of the linear equation?

$$y = \frac{1}{4}x + 3$$

(A) (B)

(C) 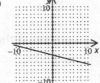 (D)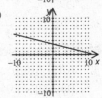

74. Which shows a graph of the linear equation?

$$y = 3$$

(A) (B)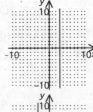

(C) 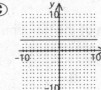 (D)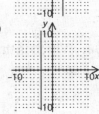

75. Which equation is represented by the graph?

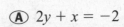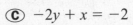

(A) $2y + x = -2$

(B) $2y - x = 2$

(C) $-2y + x = -2$

(D) $-2y - x = -2$

Georgia Diagnostic Test

76. Which shows a graph of the linear equation?

$$y - x = 2$$

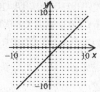

Ⓐ Ⓑ

Ⓒ Ⓓ

77. Which equation in two variables represents the values in the table?

x	−2	−1	0	1
y	7	5	3	1

Ⓐ $-4x - 2y = -6$

Ⓑ $-10x - 5y = -15$

Ⓒ $-40x - 20y = -60$

Ⓓ all of these

78. Which shows the equation of the graph in slope-intercept form?

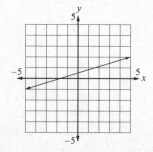

Ⓐ $y = \frac{1}{3}x + \frac{1}{2}$ Ⓑ $y = -\frac{1}{3}x + \frac{1}{2}$

Ⓒ $y = \frac{1}{3}x + 1$ Ⓓ $y = \frac{1}{3}x - \frac{1}{2}$

79. What is the value of y if the value of x is -6?

$$y = -2x - (-17)$$

Ⓐ -29

Ⓑ -25

Ⓒ -5

Ⓓ 29

80. What is the value of y if the value of x is -36?

$$y = \frac{1}{2}x - (-7)$$

Ⓐ -25

Ⓑ -11

Ⓒ 11

Ⓓ 25

81. A local train between two cities travels an average speed of 40 miles per hour. An express train leaves 2 hours later and travels at 70 mph. Which system of linear equations can be used to determine the numbers of miles, m, and the number of hours that the express train will have traveled, h, when the express train passes the local?

Ⓐ $m = 70h - 35$
   $m = 40h$

Ⓑ $m = 70h$
   $m = 40h + 80$

Ⓒ $m = 70h$
   $m = 40h + 40$

Ⓓ $m = 70h - 140$
   $m = 40h$

Georgia Diagnostic Test

82. There are two options for renting a car: pay $36 per day for unlimited mileage or pay $21 per day and 18 cents per mile. Which system of linear equations can be used to determine the number of miles for which the two options have the same cost?

(A) $y = 36x$
$\quad y = 21 + 0.18x$

(B) $y = 36x$
$\quad y = 21x + 0.18$

(C) $y = 36$
$\quad y = 21 + 0.18x$

(D) $y = 36 - 0.18x$
$\quad y = 21 + 0.18x$

83. What is the solution to this system of linear equations?
$$x + y = 5$$
$$y = 2x - 1$$

(A) $(1, 1)$

(B) $(1, 4)$

(C) $(2, 3)$

(D) $(3, 2)$

84. At what point on a graph would the lines described by these equations intersect?
$$y = 3 - x$$
$$y = x + 1$$

(A) $(-1, 4)$

(B) $(1, 2)$

(C) $(2, 1)$

(D) $(3, 4)$

85. Ralph bought 2 packs of baseball cards and 4 graphic novels for $20. Jamie bought 1 pack of baseball cards and 6 comic books, which cost $25. Which system of linear equations can be used to calculate the cost of a pack of baseball cards (b) and the cost of a graphic novel (n)?

(A) $4n + 6n = 25$
$\quad 2b + b = 20$

(B) $b + 4n = 25$
$\quad 2b + 6n = 20$

(C) $6b + n = 25$
$\quad 2b + 4n = 20$

(D) $b + 6n = 25$
$\quad 2b + 4n = 20$

86. What is the solution to this system of linear equations?
$$4x + 2y = 10$$
$$y = 3x - 5$$

(A) $(2, -1)$

(B) $(2, 1)$

(C) $(3, 4)$

(D) $(4, 3)$

Georgia Diagnostic Test

Greg asked 200 people at his gym whether they run, lift weights, or both for exercise. He made the Venn diagram to display the results. Use the Venn diagram to answer questions 87–88.

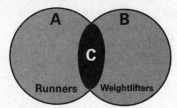

87. What does area *A* represent?

Ⓐ people who run and lift weights

Ⓑ people who only run

Ⓒ people who only lift weights

Ⓓ people who don't lift weights or run

88. If 80 people only run and 70 people only lift weights, how many people said they both run and lift weights?

Ⓐ 150   Ⓑ 50

Ⓒ 100   Ⓓ 20

89. For the sets $A = \{23, 25, 28, 33\}$ and $B = \{18, 23, 25, 35\}$, find the union of set *A* and set *B*.

Ⓐ {18, 23, 25, 28, 33, 35}

Ⓑ {18, 23, 23, 25, 25, 28, 33, 35}

Ⓒ {18, 28, 33, 35}

Ⓓ {23, 25}

90. For the sets $A = \{23, 25, 28, 33\}$ and $B = \{18, 23, 25, 35\}$, find the intersection of set *A* and set *B*.

Ⓐ {18, 23, 25, 28, 33, 35}

Ⓑ {18, 23, 23, 25, 25, 28, 33, 35}

Ⓒ {18, 28, 33, 35}

Ⓓ {23, 25}

91. For sets *A* and *B*, determine the value $A \cup B$.

$$A = \{2, 5, 8, 11, 14, 17, 22\}$$
$$B = \{3, 6, 8, 14, 15, 19, 22\}$$

Ⓐ $A \cup B = \{8, 14, 22\}$

Ⓑ $A \cup B = \{2, 5, 11, 15, 17, 19\}$

Ⓒ $A \cup B = \{2, 3, 5, 6, 8, 11, 14, 15, 17, 19, 22\}$

Ⓓ $A \cup B = \{2, 3, 5, 6, 8, 8, 11, 14, 14, 15, 17, 19, 22, 22\}$

92. For sets *A* and *B*, determine the value $A \cap B$.

$$A = \{2, 4, 6, 8, 10, 12\}$$
$$B = \{3, 6, 9, 12, 15, 18\}$$

Ⓐ $A \cap B = \{6, 12\}$

Ⓑ $A \cap B = \{2, 3, 8, 9, 10, 15, 18\}$

Ⓒ $A \cap B = \{2, 3, 4, 6, 8, 9, 10, 12, 15, 18\}$

Ⓓ $A \cap B = \{2, 3, 4, 6, 6, 8, 9, 12, 12, 15, 18\}$

Georgia Diagnostic Test

93. A coin toss can result in either heads or tails. Which diagram could be used to determine the number of possible combinations of heads and tails for 3 tosses?

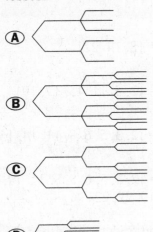

94. A box contains equal numbers of three different colors of marbles – blue, yellow, and green. The tree diagram below shows the possible combinations of drawing 2 marbles, one after the other, from the bag? How many of the combinations include at least one green marble?

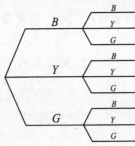

Ⓐ 3
Ⓑ 4
Ⓒ 5
Ⓓ 7

95. What is the number of possible combinations of math, science, and social studies classes that can be scheduled if the school offers 3 math options, 4 science options, and 4 social studies options?

Ⓐ 11
Ⓑ 24
Ⓒ 48
Ⓓ 64

96. What is the total number of possible combinations for abbreviations consisting of one vowel followed by two consonants? (Use 5 vowels and 21 consonants.)

Ⓐ 47
Ⓑ 105
Ⓒ 2,205
Ⓓ 4,410

Use the figure below to answer question 97.

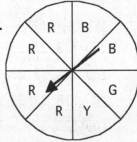

97. If you spin the spinner, what is the probability of the pointer landing on *R*?

Ⓐ $\frac{1}{4}$

Ⓑ 1

Ⓒ $\frac{1}{2}$

Ⓓ $\frac{3}{8}$

Georgia Diagnostic Test

98. A number cube with the numbers 1 through 6 is rolled. Find the probability of rolling the number 4.

Ⓐ $\frac{1}{3}$

Ⓑ 1

Ⓒ $\frac{1}{6}$

Ⓓ $\frac{5}{6}$

99. A bag contains 40 red marbles, 20 yellow marbles, and 20 green marbles. What is the probability of drawing one red marble and one yellow marble in two draws, if the first marble is replaced before the second draw?

Ⓐ $\frac{1}{2}$

Ⓑ $\frac{1}{8}$

Ⓒ $\frac{1}{16}$

Ⓓ $\frac{1}{800}$

100. What is the probability of rolling all sixes on a single roll of 3 dice?

Ⓐ $\frac{1}{2}$

Ⓑ $\frac{1}{6}$

Ⓒ $\frac{1}{36}$

Ⓓ $\frac{1}{216}$

101. A highway engineer collected data on a repair project. The table and the scatter plot below show the comparison of cost of materials and the length of the repaired road segment. Which analysis best describes the data?

Length (meters)	500	1000	1500	2000	2500	3000
Cost ($ thousands)	40	80	120	160	200	240

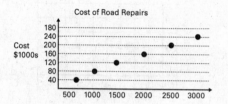

Cost of Road Repairs

Ⓐ The cost is not a function of the length of the repair.

Ⓑ The cost increases as a linear function of the length of the repair.

Ⓒ The cost decreases as a linear function of the length of the repair.

Ⓓ The cost increases as a nonlinear function of the length of the repair.

Diagnostic Test

Georgia Diagnostic Test

102. The scatter plot shows the relationship between the number of years a company was in business and the number of employees. Which is the best conclusion based on the plot?

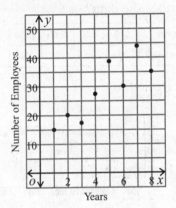

(A) the number of employees stayed the same from year to year

(B) the number of employees increased each year

(C) the number of employees tended to decrease over time

(D) the number of employees tended to increase over time

103. Estimate the line of best fit for this scatter plot.

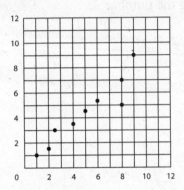

(A) $y = 3x$

(B) $y = x + 1$

(C) $y = x + 3$

(D) $y = 2x + 3$

104. Estimate the line of best fit for this scatter plot.

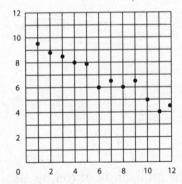

(A) $y = -2x + 10$

(B) $y = -x + 10$

(C) $y = -0.5x + 10$

(D) $y = x + 10$

M8N1.a

Find square roots of perfect squares.

MULTIPLE CHOICE

1. Which of these numbers is a square root of 49?

   Ⓐ 6

   Ⓑ 7

   Ⓒ 8

   Ⓓ 9

2. Which of these numbers is the same as $\sqrt{81}$?

   Ⓐ −9

   Ⓑ −6

   Ⓒ 8

   Ⓓ 11

3. What is the square root?
$$\sqrt{\frac{25}{64}}$$

   Ⓐ $\frac{1}{6}$

   Ⓑ $\frac{5}{8}$

   Ⓒ $\frac{1}{8}$

   Ⓓ $\frac{1}{12}$

4. Which shows the square root?
$$\sqrt{\frac{9}{36}}$$

   Ⓐ $\frac{1}{6}$

   Ⓑ $\frac{5}{8}$

   Ⓒ $\frac{1}{2}$

   Ⓓ $\frac{1}{12}$

5. Which of these numbers is a solution to the square root $\sqrt{0.36}$?

   Ⓐ 0.006

   Ⓑ 0.06

   Ⓒ 0.6

   Ⓓ 6.0

6. What is the square root to the nearest tenth? (You may use a calculator.)
$$-\sqrt{0.81}$$

   Ⓐ −0.45

   Ⓑ −0.045

   Ⓒ −0.9

   Ⓓ −0.09

GPS Practice Pages

7. Evaluate. $\sqrt{36x^2}$

    Ⓐ 6

    Ⓑ $6x$

    Ⓒ $6x^2$

    Ⓓ $36x$

8. Which of the following has the same value?

$$\sqrt{x^2y^6}$$

    Ⓐ $3xy$

    Ⓑ xy^2

    Ⓒ $3xy^2$

    Ⓓ xy^3

M8N1.b

Recognize the (positive) square root of a number as a length of a side of a square with a given area.

MULTIPLE CHOICE

1. What is the length of the side of a square that has an area of 144 cm²?

   Ⓐ 12 cm

   Ⓑ 14 cm

   Ⓒ 18 cm

   Ⓓ 24 cm

2. What is the area of this square?

   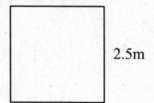
   2.5m

   Ⓐ 6.25m²

   Ⓑ 8m²

   Ⓒ 10m²

   Ⓓ 12.5m²

3. What is the side length of a square having the given area?

   $$A = 169 \text{ ft.}^2$$

   Ⓐ 3.25 ft.

   Ⓑ 6.5 ft.

   Ⓒ 13 ft.

   Ⓓ 42.25 ft.

4. Mary's garden plot is a square with an area of 82 ft². What is the approximate length of one side of Mary's garden?

   Ⓐ 6 ft.

   Ⓑ 8 ft.

   Ⓒ 9 ft.

   Ⓓ 11 ft.

5. What is the length of the side of a square with an area of 0.01 m²?

   Ⓐ 0.01 m

   Ⓑ 0.0̄3 m

   Ⓒ 0.1 m

   Ⓓ 0.3̄ m

6. What is the area of this square?

   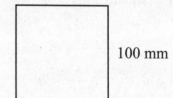
   100 mm

   Ⓐ 10 mm²

   Ⓑ 1,000 mm²

   Ⓒ 10,000 mm²

   Ⓓ 100,000 mm²

GPS Practice Pages

7. What is the value of t if the area of the square is 64 square units?

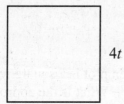

4t

Ⓐ 2 units

Ⓑ 4 units

Ⓒ 8 units

Ⓓ 16 units

8. What is the area of this square?

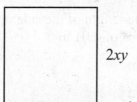

2xy

Ⓐ 4xy square units

Ⓑ 16xy square units

Ⓒ 2x^2y^2 square units

Ⓓ 4x^2y^2 square units

M8N1.c

Recognize square roots as points and as lengths on a number line.

MULTIPLE CHOICE

1. Which point on the number line represents $\sqrt{64}$?

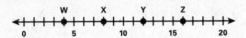

- Ⓐ point W
- Ⓑ point X
- Ⓒ point Y
- Ⓓ point Z

2. Which point(s) on the number line represent(s) $-\sqrt{36}$?

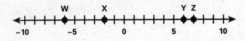

- Ⓐ point W only
- Ⓑ point Y only
- Ⓒ point Z only
- Ⓓ point W and point Y

3. Which point on the number line represents $\sqrt{\dfrac{25}{81}}$?

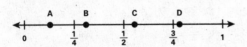

- Ⓐ point A
- Ⓑ point B
- Ⓒ point C
- Ⓓ point D

4. Which point on the number line represents $\sqrt{0.25}$?

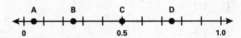

- Ⓐ point A
- Ⓑ point B
- Ⓒ point C
- Ⓓ point D

5. Match the point on the line with the correct number below.

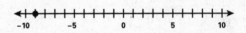

- Ⓐ $\sqrt{-81}$
- Ⓑ $\sqrt{-9}$
- Ⓒ $\sqrt{9}$
- Ⓓ $\sqrt{81}$

6. Use the number line to determine the length between the two points that are represented by $\sqrt{9}$.

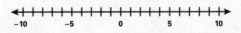

- Ⓐ 3
- Ⓑ 6
- Ⓒ 9
- Ⓓ 12

7. Use the number line to determine the length between the positive $\sqrt{16}$ and the negative $\sqrt{100}$.

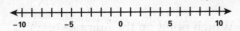

Ⓐ 6

Ⓑ 10

Ⓒ 12

Ⓓ 14

8. Round $\sqrt{95}$ to the nearest whole number to determine which point on the number line corresponds to $\sqrt{95}$.

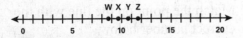

Ⓐ W

Ⓑ X

Ⓒ Y

Ⓓ Z

GPS Practice Pages

M8N1.d

Understand that the square root of 0 is 0 and that every positive number has two square roots that are opposite in sign.

MULTIPLE CHOICE

1. What is the value of the expression?
$$\sqrt{10^2} - 10$$

(A) -10

(B) 0

(C) 10

(D) 100

2. Which statement below best describes the number statement?
$$\sqrt{81} = 9$$

(A) always true

(B) never true

(C) sometimes true

(D) cannot be determined

3. Which statement below best describes the number statement?
$$-\sqrt{576} = 24$$

(A) always true

(B) never true

(C) sometimes true

(D) cannot be determined

4. Which choice below best describes the expression?
$$\sqrt{0.0225}$$

(A) 0.015

(B) -0.015 or 0.015

(C) 0.15

(D) -0.15 or 0.15

5. What is the square root? $-\sqrt{\dfrac{1}{16}}$

(A) -4

(B) $-\dfrac{1}{4}$

(C) $\dfrac{1}{256}$

(D) 0.4

6. Which of the following best describes the statement?
$$\sqrt{9 \times 9} = 9$$

(A) always true

(B) never true

(C) sometimes true

(D) cannot be determined

GPS Practice Pages

7. Which of the following is not equivalent to the square root?

$$\sqrt{\dfrac{4}{100}}$$

(A) -0.2

(B) $-\dfrac{4}{10}$

(C) $\dfrac{1}{5}$

(D) $\dfrac{\sqrt{4}}{\sqrt{100}}$

8. Which of the following is not equal to the value of this square root?

$$\sqrt{(3^2)(4^4)}$$

(A) -48

(B) $-(3^2)(4^2)$

(C) $(3)(4^2)$

(D) 48

M8N1.e

Recognize and use the radical symbol to denote the positive square root of a positive number.

MULTIPLE CHOICE

1. Two streets that are the same width intersect. If the area of the intersection is 484 square feet, how can you calculate the width of the streets?

   Ⓐ $\sqrt{484} = 22$

   Ⓑ $\sqrt{484} = -22$

   Ⓒ $\sqrt{484} = -22$ or 22

   Ⓓ $\sqrt{484} = \sqrt{22}$

2. Evaluate. $\sqrt{961^2}$

   Ⓐ 31

   Ⓑ 39

   Ⓒ 961

   Ⓓ 923,521

3. Evaluate the positive square root indicated by the symbol. $\sqrt{0.04}$

   Ⓐ 0.002

   Ⓑ 0.02

   Ⓒ 0.16

   Ⓓ 0.20

4. Which of the number statements is accurate?

   Ⓐ $-\sqrt{9} = -3$

   Ⓑ $-\sqrt{9} = -81$

   Ⓒ $-\sqrt{9} = 81$

   Ⓓ $-\sqrt{3} = -9$

5. Use the value of $\sqrt{729}$ to determine the side length of a pillow with a front that is a square piece of fabric with an area of 729 square inches.

   Ⓐ −29 inches

   Ⓑ −27 inches

   Ⓒ 27 inches

   Ⓓ 29 inches

6. Evaluate. $\sqrt{\dfrac{36}{100}}$

   Ⓐ 0.30

   Ⓑ $0.3\overline{3}$

   Ⓒ 0.36

   Ⓓ 0.60

GPS Practice Pages

7. What is the positive square root? $\sqrt{\dfrac{1}{y^6}}$

(A) y^2

(B) y^3

(C) $\dfrac{1}{y^3}$

(D) y^{-6}

8. Evaluate. $\sqrt{4x^2y^{16}}$

(A) $2xy^4$

(B) $2xy^8$

(C) $4xy^8$

(D) $16xy^4$

M8N1.f
Estimate square roots of positive numbers.

MULTIPLE CHOICE

1. What is the approximate square root to the nearest whole number? $\sqrt{83}$

   (A) 8

   (B) 9

   (C) 9.1

   (D) 10

2. What is the approximate square root to the nearest whole number? $\sqrt{149}$

   (A) 12

   (B) 14

   (C) 17

   (D) 19

3. The formula $\sqrt{64h}$ can be used to find the velocity, v, in feet per second of an object that has fallen h feet. Estimate the velocity of an object that has fallen 35 feet to the nearest foot per second.

   (A) 6

   (B) 48

   (C) 384

   (D) 2,240

4. You want to find the length of your back yard. You know that the yard is square and has an area of 870 square feet. Without using a calculator, what is the approximate length of the back yard?

   (A) 15 feet

   (B) 27 feet

   (C) 30 feet

   (D) 34 feet

5. Without using a calculator, approximate the square root to the nearest hundredth. $\sqrt{0.0395}$

   (A) 0.02

   (B) 0.06

   (C) 0.15

   (D) 0.20

6. Without using a calculator, approximate the square root. $\sqrt{0.0000989}$

   (A) 0.1

   (B) 0.01

   (C) 0.001

   (D) 0.0001

7. What is the approximate square root?

$$\sqrt{\frac{25}{398}}$$

Ⓐ $\frac{1}{16}$

Ⓑ $\frac{1}{8}$

Ⓒ $\frac{1}{4}$

Ⓓ $\frac{5}{8}$

8. What is the approximate square root?

$$\sqrt{\frac{x}{98}}$$

Ⓐ $\frac{1}{10}x$

Ⓑ $\frac{1}{10}\sqrt{x}$

Ⓒ $\frac{1}{9}\sqrt{x}$

Ⓓ $\frac{1}{8}\sqrt{x}$

M8N1.g
Simplify, add, subtract, multiply, and divide expressions containing square roots.

MULTIPLE CHOICE

1. Express this number in the simplest form.
$$\sqrt{2 \times 8}$$
   - (A) $4\sqrt{2}$
   - (B) 4
   - (C) $\sqrt{16}$
   - (D) 8

2. Evaluate. $\sqrt{\dfrac{500}{125}}$
   - (A) 2
   - (B) 4
   - (C) 20
   - (D) 40

3. Express this number in the simplest form.
$$5\sqrt{16}$$
   - (A) $10\sqrt{2}$
   - (B) 20
   - (C) 80
   - (D) $\sqrt{80}$

4. Evaluate. $\sqrt{400} + \sqrt{4}$
   - (A) 10
   - (B) 20.2
   - (C) 22
   - (D) $\sqrt{404}$

5. Evaluate. $\sqrt{100} - \sqrt{64}$
   - (A) 2
   - (B) 4
   - (C) 6
   - (D) 8

6. Evaluate. $3\sqrt{25} + 5\sqrt{9}$
   - (A) 9
   - (B) 15
   - (C) 18
   - (D) 30

GPS Practice Pages

7. Evaluate. $\sqrt{4x^2} + \sqrt{4x^2}$

Ⓐ $4x$

Ⓑ $4x\sqrt{2}$

Ⓒ $4x^2$

Ⓓ $2x^4$

8. Evaluate. $3x^2\sqrt{4x^2}$

Ⓐ $6x^3$

Ⓑ $12x^3$

Ⓒ $6x^4$

Ⓓ $12x^4$

M8N1.h

Distinguish between rational and irrational numbers.

MULTIPLE CHOICE

1. Which number is irrational?

(A) $\frac{1}{17}$

(B) 3.1415926 ...

(C) $-\sqrt{121}$

(D) $5.43\overline{24}$

2. Which number is rational?

(A) 8.18811888111 ...

(B) $\sqrt{102}$

(C) $1\frac{3}{5}$

(D) $\sqrt{110}$

3. Which number is irrational?

(A) 0.121243486 ...

(B) 7.7778

(C) $\sqrt{81}$

(D) $\frac{3}{8}$

4. Which number is irrational?

(A) -31.1357

(B) $\sqrt{128}$

(C) $-\sqrt{196}$

(D) $\frac{1}{17}$

5. Which number is irrational?

(A) $\frac{4}{27}$

(B) $6.\overline{66}$

(C) $\sqrt{225}$

(D) $-\sqrt{2}$

6. Which of the following is a rational number?

(A) $-\sqrt{\frac{1}{7}}$

(B) $-\sqrt{\frac{1}{64}}$

(C) $\sqrt{\frac{1}{17}}$

(D) $\sqrt{\frac{1}{26}}$

GPS Practice Pages

7. For which value of x is $\sqrt{5x}$ a rational number?

(A) 0

(B) 1

(C) 2

(D) 8

8. For which value of x is $\sqrt{\dfrac{72}{x}}$ a rational number?

(A) 0

(B) 1

(C) 2

(D) 36

GPS Practice Pages

M8N1.i

Simplify expressions containing integer exponents.

MULTIPLE CHOICE

1. Simplify the expression.

$$3x^2 + 4x + 5x + 6x^2$$

Ⓐ $18x$

Ⓑ $18x^2 + 20x$

Ⓒ $9x^2 + 9x$

Ⓓ $18x^2$

2. What is the value of the expression for the given value of a?

$$a^3 \text{ when } a = 4$$

Ⓐ 16

Ⓑ 32

Ⓒ 12

Ⓓ 64

3. Simplify the expression.

$$-3y - 5y^2 + 6 - 4y^2 + 6y^3$$

Ⓐ $6y^3 - y^2 - 3y + 6$

Ⓑ $-3y^2 - 3y + 6$

Ⓒ $6y^3 + 9y^2 - 3y + 6$

Ⓓ $6y^3 - 9y^2 - 3y + 6$

4. Simplify the expression.

$$4x^2 + 4x + x(x)$$

Ⓐ $4x^2 + 5x$

Ⓑ $x^3 + 5x^2 + 4x$

Ⓒ $5x^2 + 4x$

Ⓓ $5x^2 + 5x$

5. Simplify the expression.

$$8a^2 + 4a + b^2 + 3 - 12a$$

Ⓐ $8a^2 - 8a + b^2 + 3$

Ⓑ $8a^2 + 8a + b^2 + 3$

Ⓒ $9a^2 - 8a + 3$

Ⓓ $8a^2 \; 16a + b^2 + 3$

6. Simplify the expression.

$$(3x^2)(2x) + (4x)(5x) + 6x^2$$

Ⓐ $5x^3 + 6x^2 + 20x$

Ⓑ $26x^3 + 6x^2$

Ⓒ $36x^3 + 26x^2$

Ⓓ $6x^3 + 26x^2$

GPS Practice Pages

7. Simplify the expression.
$$3x^2 + 7x^2 + 5x^3$$

Ⓐ $5x^3 + 10x^2$

Ⓑ $5x^3 + 10x^4$

Ⓒ $5x^3 + 21x^2$

Ⓓ $15\,x^7$

8. Simplify the expression.
$$(4y)(y^2) + y^3 + y^2$$

Ⓐ $y^3 + 5y^2 + 4y$

Ⓑ $y^3 + 5y^2$

Ⓒ $4y^3 + y^2$

Ⓓ $5y^3 + y^2$

M8N1.j
Express and use numbers in scientific notation.

MULTIPLE CHOICE

1. What is 0.000659 written in scientific notation?

   Ⓐ 0.659×10^{-3}

   Ⓑ 6.59×10^{-3}

   Ⓒ 6.59×10^{-4}

   Ⓓ 659×10^{-6}

2. What is 1.93×10^3 written in standard form?

   Ⓐ 193

   Ⓑ 1,930

   Ⓒ 19,300

   Ⓓ 193,000

3. What is 9.91×10^7 written in standard form?

   Ⓐ 0.000000991

   Ⓑ 9,910,000

   Ⓒ 991,000,000

   Ⓓ 99,100,000

4. What is 0.78 written in scientific notation?

   Ⓐ 0.78×10^3

   Ⓑ 7.8×10^1

   Ⓒ 78×10^4

   Ⓓ 7.8×1^{-1}

5. Which is least?

   Ⓐ 8.14×10^4

   Ⓑ 8.41×10^5

   Ⓒ 8.0014×10^3

   Ⓓ 8.401×10^4

6. The diameter of a red blood cell is 0.0065 centimeters. What is this diameter in scientific notation?

   Ⓐ 6.5×10^{-4} cm

   Ⓑ 65×10^{-4} cm

   Ⓒ 6.5×10^{-3} cm

   Ⓓ 6.5×10^{-2} cm

GPS Practice Pages

7. The planet Saturn travels 1,429,400,000 kilometers each time it orbits the sun. What is the distance of Saturn's orbit in scientific notation?

- (A) 1.4294×10^5 km
- (B) $14,294 \times 10^5$ km
- (C) 1.4294×10^8 km
- (D) 1.4294×10^9 km

8. The graph shows the national debt for the United States from 1980 to 2000. What was the national debt in 2000?

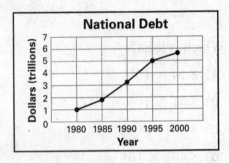

- (A) $$5.6 \times 10^{12}$$
- (B) $$5.6 \times 10^{11}$$
- (C) $$5.6 \times 10^{10}$$
- (D) $$5.6 \times 10^{9}$$

M8N1.k

Use appropriate technologies to solve problems involving square roots, exponents, and scientific notation.

MULTIPLE CHOICE

1. To the nearest tenth, what is the value of $\sqrt{55}$? (You may use a calculator.)

    Ⓐ 6.9

    Ⓑ 7.4

    Ⓒ 7.9

    Ⓓ 8.3

2. To the nearest hundredth, what is the value of $\sqrt{5 \times 7}$?
   (You may use a calculator.)

    Ⓐ 5.92

    Ⓑ 6.00

    Ⓒ 6.52

    Ⓓ 7.10

3. To the nearest thousandth, what is the value of $\sqrt{0.0079}$?
   (You may use a calculator.)

    Ⓐ 0.023

    Ⓑ 0.089

    Ⓒ 0.231

    Ⓓ 0.887

4. To the nearest tenth, what is the value of $\sqrt{10^3}$? (You may use a calculator.)

    Ⓐ 10.0

    Ⓑ 31.6

    Ⓒ 63.2

    Ⓓ 100.0

5. What is the value of the expression?
   (You may use a calculator.)
   $$2^4 \times 3^3 \times 5^0$$

    Ⓐ 432

    Ⓑ 864

    Ⓒ 1,296

    Ⓓ 2,160

6. Evaluate the expression for $x = 9$.
   (You may use a calculator.)
   $$x^3 + x^2 + \sqrt{x}$$

    Ⓐ 165

    Ⓑ 732

    Ⓒ 810

    Ⓓ 813

GPS Practice Pages

7. Calculate the product. (You may use a calculator.)

$$(1.3 \times 10^2) \times (5.6 \times 10^3)$$

Ⓐ 4.31×10^3

Ⓑ 7.28×10^4

Ⓒ 7.28×10^5

Ⓓ 7.28×10^6

8. For which value of x is $\sqrt{5x}$ approximately 11.8?
(You may use a calculator.)

Ⓐ 2.4

Ⓑ 5.6

Ⓒ 16

Ⓓ 28

GPS Practice Pages

M8G1.a

Investigate characteristics of parallel and perpendicular lines both algebraically and geometrically.

MULTIPLE CHOICE

1. Which of the following statements is true of perpendicular lines?

  Ⓐ (slope of line a)(slope of line b) = (slope of line a)^2

  Ⓑ (slope of line a)(slope of line b) = 1

  Ⓒ (slope of line a)(slope of line b) = -1

  Ⓓ (slope of line a)(slope of line b) = 0

2. Which of these equations describes a line that is parallel to $y = 5x + 23$?

  Ⓐ $y = 5x + 18$

  Ⓑ $y = -5x + 23$

  Ⓒ $y = \frac{1}{5}x + 23$

  Ⓓ $y = \frac{1}{5}x + 18$

3. Which of these equations describes a line that is perpendicular to $y = 2x - 14$?

  Ⓐ $y = 2x + 14$

  Ⓑ $y = 0.5x + 14$

  Ⓒ $y = -0.5x + 14$

  Ⓓ $y = 0.5x - 14$

4. Which of the following lines is parallel to $y = 4x + 3$?

  Ⓐ $y = -4x - 3$

  Ⓑ $y = -4x + 3$

  Ⓒ $y = -\frac{1}{4}x + 3$

  Ⓓ $y = 4x - 3$

5. Which of the following lines is perpendicular to $y = -3x + 8$?

  Ⓐ $y = -\frac{1}{3}x + 8$

  Ⓑ $y = \frac{1}{3}x + 8$

  Ⓒ $y = 3x + 8$

  Ⓓ $y = 8x - 8$

6. Which of these equations describes a line that is perpendicular to the line shown in the graph?

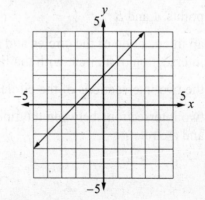

  Ⓐ $y = x - 2$

  Ⓑ $y = 2 - x$

  Ⓒ $y = 2x + 2$

  Ⓓ $y = 2 - 2x$

7. Which of these equations describes a line that is parallel to the line shown in the graph?

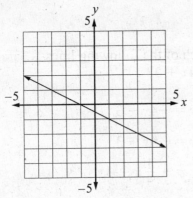

Ⓐ $y = 2x + 2$

Ⓑ $y = -2x + 2$

Ⓒ $y = \frac{1}{2}x - 32$

Ⓒ $y = -\frac{1}{2}x - 32$

8. If A and B are the center points of the circles, a line perpendicular to $\overleftrightarrow{AB}$ can be drawn by connecting what two points?

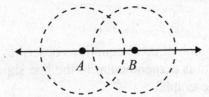

Ⓐ points A and B

Ⓑ an intersection of the circles and an intersection of a circle with the line

Ⓒ the two intersections of the circles

Ⓓ two intersections between the line and a circle

M8G1.b

Apply properties of angle pairs formed by parallel lines cut by a transversal.

MULTIPLE CHOICE

1. If lines *a* and *b* are parallel, which pair of angles have equal measures?

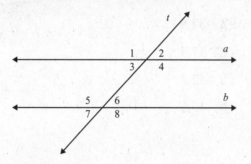

- Ⓐ ∠1 and ∠2
- Ⓑ ∠1 and ∠3
- Ⓒ ∠1 and ∠7
- Ⓓ ∠1 and ∠8

2. If lines *a* and *b* are parallel and $m\angle 2 = 40°$, what is $m\angle 5$?

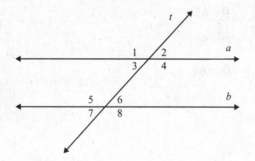

- Ⓐ 40°
- Ⓑ 50°
- Ⓒ 140°
- Ⓓ 180°

3. If lines *a* and *b* are parallel, find the measure of angle 3.

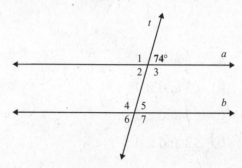

- Ⓐ $m\angle 3 = 74°$
- Ⓑ $m\angle 3 = 106°$
- Ⓒ $m\angle 3 = 116°$
- Ⓓ $m\angle 3 = 174°$

4. If lines *a* and *b* are parallel, which of the following is *not* true?

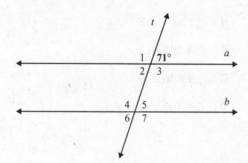

- Ⓐ $m\angle 6 = 71°$
- Ⓑ $m\angle 5 = 109°$
- Ⓒ $m\angle 2 = 71°$
- Ⓓ $m\angle 4 = 109°$

GPS Practice Pages

5. Which pair of angles are alternate interior angles?

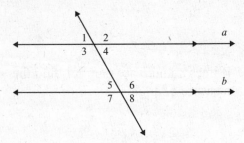

- (A) ∠2 and ∠7
- (B) ∠3 and ∠4
- (C) ∠3 and ∠5
- (D) ∠3 and ∠6

6. Which angles are corresponding angles?

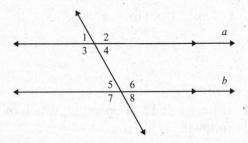

- (A) ∠1 and ∠8
- (B) ∠4 and ∠5
- (C) ∠4 and ∠6
- (D) ∠4 and ∠8

7. What is the value of x?

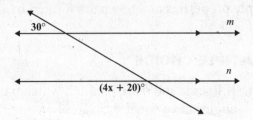

- (A) 32.5
- (B) 37.5
- (C) 42.5
- (D) 47.5

8. What is the value of x?

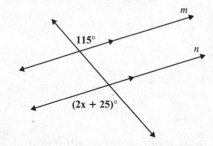

- (A) 25
- (B) 45
- (C) 50
- (D) 90

M8G1.c

Understand the properties of the ratio of segments of parallel lines cut by one or more transversals.

MULTIPLE CHOICE

1. In this diagram, which lines(s) are transversals?

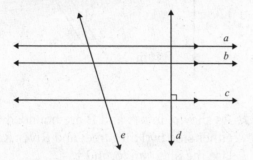

   (A) lines *a, b,* and *c*

   (B) line *b* only

   (C) lines *d* and *e*

   (D) line *e* only

2. Which lines are parallel?

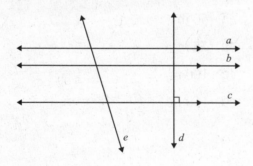

   (A) lines *a, b,* and *c*

   (B) line *b* only

   (C) lines *b* and *c* only

   (D) lines *d* and *c*

3. For the figure below, which statement is *not* necessarily true?

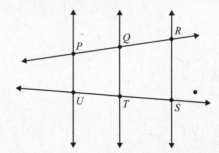

   (A) $\dfrac{PQ}{QR} = \dfrac{UT}{TS}$

   (B) $\dfrac{QR}{RS} = \dfrac{TS}{RS}$

   (C) $\dfrac{TS}{UT} = \dfrac{QR}{PQ}$

   (D) $\dfrac{PQ}{PR} = \dfrac{UT}{US}$

4. Find the value of *x*.

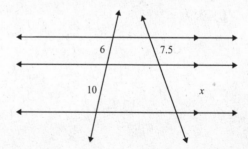

   (A) 9

   (B) 10.5

   (C) 12.5

   (D) 15

GPS Practice Pages

5. Find the length of $\overline{AB}$.

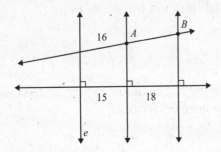

  (A) 18

  (B) 18.2

  (C) 19

  (D) 19.2

6. Find the value of x.

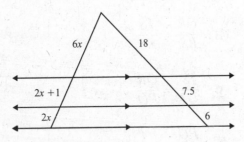

  (A) $\dfrac{1}{2}$

  (B) 1

  (C) 2

  (D) 3

Use this illustration to answer questions 7 and 8.

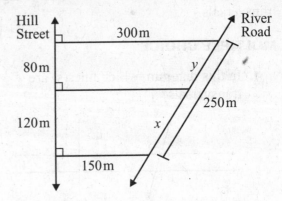

7. As shown, lots A and B are bounded on either side by Hill Street and River Road. Use the diagram to find x.

  (A) 100 m

  (B) 150 m

  (C) 175 m

  (D) 200 m

8. Find the value of y.

  (A) 50 m

  (B) 75 m

  (C) 100 m

  (D) 150 m

M8G1.d

Understand the meaning of congruence: that all corresponding angles are congruent and all corresponding sides are congruent.

MULTIPLE CHOICE

1. Determine which triangle is congruent to the given triangle.

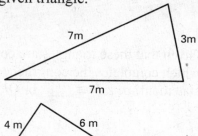

Ⓐ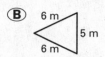

Ⓑ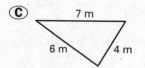

Ⓒ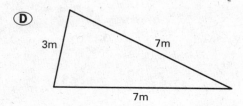

Ⓓ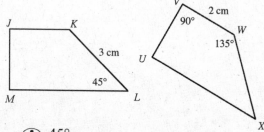

2. Quadrilateral $JKLM \cong$ quadrilateral $VWXU$. What is the measure of $m\angle K$?

Ⓐ 45°

Ⓑ 90°

Ⓒ 135°

Ⓓ 180°

3. How do you know that the triangles are congruent? Which equation can be used to solve for x?

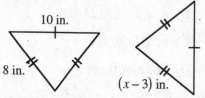

Ⓐ Side-Angle-Side; $x - 3 = 8$, 11 in.

Ⓑ Side-Side-Side; $x - 3 = 8$, 11 in.

Ⓒ Side-Side-Side; $x - 3 = 8$, 5 in.

Ⓓ Side-Angle-Side; $x - 3 = 8$, 5 in.

4. How do you know that the triangles are congruent? Which equation can be used to solve for x?

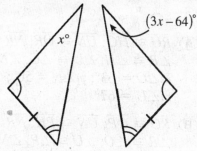

Ⓐ SAS; $x = 3x - 64$; 32

Ⓑ SAS; $x = 3x - 64$; 16

Ⓒ ASA; $x = 3x - 64$; 16

Ⓓ ASA; $x = 3x - 64$; 32

GPS Practice Pages

5. △*OPT* is congruent to △*IDL*. Which completes the congruence statement?
a. ∠*T* ≅ ____   b. $\overline{TO}$ ≅ ____

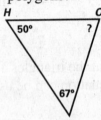

Ⓐ a. ∠*L*   b. $\overline{LI}$

Ⓑ a. ∠*L*   b. $\overline{LD}$

Ⓒ a. ∠*I*   b. $\overline{ID}$

Ⓓ none of these

6. Which shows the corresponding sides, the corresponding angles, and the unknown measures of the congruent polygons?

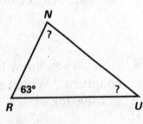

Ⓐ $\overline{RU} \cong \overline{HO}$; $\overline{UN} \cong \overline{OP}$; $\overline{NR} \cong \overline{PH}$;
∠*R* ≅ ∠*H*; ∠*U* ≅ ∠*O*; ∠*N* ≅ ∠*P*;
m∠*O* = 63°; *m*∠*N* = 50°;
m∠*U* = 67°

Ⓑ $\overline{RU} \cong \overline{OP}$; $\overline{UN} \cong \overline{PH}$; $\overline{NR} \cong \overline{HO}$;
∠*R* ≅ ∠*O*; ∠*U* ≅ ∠*P*; ∠*N* ≅ ∠*H*;
m∠*O* = 63°; *m*∠*N* = 50°;
m∠*U* = 67°

Ⓒ $\overline{RU} \cong \overline{OH}$; $\overline{UN} \cong \overline{HP}$; $\overline{NR} \cong \overline{PO}$;
∠*R* ≅ ∠*O*; ∠*U* ≅ ∠*H*; ∠*N* ≅ ∠*P*;
m∠*O* = 63°; *m*∠*N* = 67°;
m∠*U* = 50°

Ⓓ $\overline{RU} \cong \overline{OH}$; $\overline{UN} \cong \overline{HP}$; $\overline{NR} \cong \overline{PO}$;
∠*R* ≅ ∠*O*; ∠*U* ≅ ∠*H*; ∠*N* ≅ ∠*P*;
m∠*O* = 63°; *m*∠*N* = 50°;
m∠*U* = 67°

7. Which statement is true?

Ⓐ All circles are congruent.

Ⓑ All parallelograms are similar.

Ⓒ All squares are congruent.

Ⓓ All regular hexagons are similar.

8. Given that these triangles are congruent, which completes the congruence statement? a. ∠*P* ≅ ____   b. $\overline{OP}$ ≅ ____

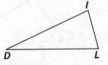
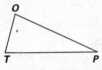

Ⓐ a. ∠*D*   b. $\overline{IL}$

Ⓑ a. ∠*D*   b. $\overline{ID}$

Ⓒ a. ∠*D*   b. $\overline{DL}$

Ⓓ none of these

GPS Practice Pages

M8G2.a

Apply properties of right triangles, including the Pythagorean Theorem.

MULTIPLE CHOICE

1. What is the value of a?

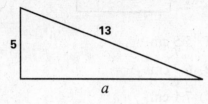

- **A** 5
- **B** 8
- **C** 11
- **D** 12

2. What is the measure of $\angle x$?

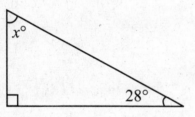

- **A** 28°
- **B** 62°
- **C** 72°
- **D** 90°

3. What is the length of c? Round to the nearest hundredth, if necessary.

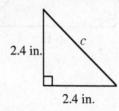

- **A** 2.19 in.
- **B** 2.86 in.
- **C** 3.39 in.
- **D** 4.80 in.

4. Which triangle with the given side lengths is a right triangle?

- **A** $a = 8$ in., $b = 24$ in., $c = 26$ in.
- **B** $a = 12$ in., $b = 16$ in., $c = 20$ in.
- **C** $a = 7$ in., $b = 24$ in., $c = 25$ in.
- **D** $a = 7$ in., $b = 23$ in., $c = 25$ in.

5. Which set of numbers is not a Pythagorean triple?

- **A** 20, 48, 52
- **B** 11, 24, 26
- **C** 10, 24, 26
- **D** 5, 12, 13

GPS Practice Pages

6. What is the value of x?

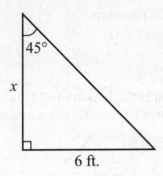

45°

x

6 ft.

Ⓐ 6 ft.

Ⓑ 8 ft.

Ⓒ 10 ft.

Ⓓ 16 ft.

7. The size of a rectangular computer monitor is given by it diagonal. To the nearest inch what is the width of a 22 inch monitor that is 11 inches high?

Ⓐ 11 inches

Ⓑ 15 inches

Ⓒ 19 inches

Ⓓ 33 inches

8. To the nearest tenth, what is the diagonal of this square?

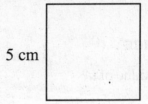

5 cm

Ⓐ 5.5 cm

Ⓑ 6.7 cm

Ⓒ 7.1 cm

Ⓓ 10.0 cm

M8G2.b

Recognize and interpret the Pythagorean Theorem as a statement about areas of squares on the sides of a right triangle.

MULTIPLE CHOICE

1. What is the area of square *ABCD*?

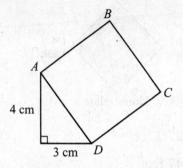

4 cm
3 cm

Ⓐ 9 cm²

Ⓑ 16 cm²

Ⓒ 25 cm²

Ⓓ 49 cm²

2. If the area of square *ABCD* is 6.25 in.², what is the area of square *AEFG*?

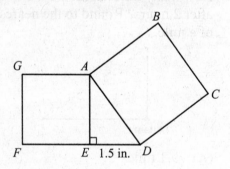

E 1.5 in.

Ⓐ 2 in.²

Ⓑ 2.5 in.²

Ⓒ 4 in.²

Ⓓ 6.25 in.²

3. If the area of square *AEFG* is 16 m², what is the area of square *ABCD*?

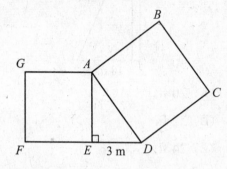

E 3 m

Ⓐ 20 m²

Ⓑ 25 m²

Ⓒ 36 m²

Ⓓ 49 m²

4. What is the length of the diagonal of this rectangle?

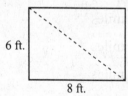

6 ft.
8 ft.

Ⓐ 9 ft.

Ⓑ 10 ft.

Ⓒ 12 ft.

Ⓓ 14 ft.

GPS Practice Pages

5. A support cable for a utility pole runs from the top of the pole to a point 10 feet from its base. If the cable is 26 meters long, how tall is the pole?

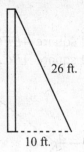

26 ft.

10 ft.

  Ⓐ 20 ft.

  Ⓑ 22 ft.

  Ⓒ 24 ft.

  Ⓓ 28 ft.

6. A boat in the ocean is 120 miles directly north of a small island. The boat begins to head to shore but is pushed by a wind heading directly east. The boat ends up 50 miles directly east of the island. If the boat traveled in a straight line, how many miles did it travel?

  Ⓐ 130 miles

  Ⓑ 145 miles

  Ⓒ 155 miles

  Ⓓ 170 miles

7. A baseball diamond is a square measuring 90 feet from one base to the next. How long is the throw from first base to third base? Round to the nearest tenth of a foot.

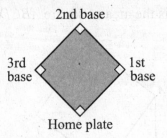

2nd base

3rd base   1st base

Home plate

  Ⓐ 127.3 feet

  Ⓑ 147 feet

  Ⓒ 155.5 feet

  Ⓓ 180 feet

8. Two cars leave Atlanta, Georgia at the same time. One travels directly north at a rate of 45 miles per hour and the other travels directly east at 65 miles per hour. How many miles apart are the two cars after 2 hours? Round to the nearest tenth of a mile.

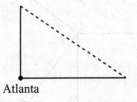

Atlanta

  Ⓐ 79.1 miles

  Ⓑ 100.0 miles

  Ⓒ 158.1 miles.

  Ⓓ 220.0 miles

GPS Practice Pages

M8A1.a

Represent a given situation using algebraic expressions or equations in one variable.

MULTIPLE CHOICE

1. Let y represent the number. Which variable expression represents the verbal expression? The sum of $\frac{1}{4}$ of a number and 120 is 315.

   (A) $\frac{1}{4}y + 120 = 315$

   (B) $y\left(\frac{1}{4} + 120\right) = 315$

   (C) $\frac{1}{4} + 120y = 315$

   (D) $\frac{1}{4}(y + 120) = 315$

2. Let y represent the number. Which variable expression represents the verbal expression?
   The difference of -8 and a number is -51.

   (A) $y + (-8) = -51$

   (B) $-8 - y = 51$

   (C) $-51 - y = -8$

   (D) $-51 - (-8) = y$

3. Let t represent the number. Which variable expression represents the verbal expression?
   4 fewer cans than Tom collected

   (A) $4t$

   (B) $\frac{t}{4}$

   (C) $t - 4$

   (D) $t + 4$

4. Which shows the statement translated into an equation, along with the solution? The sum of 8 and 3 times a number is 23.

   (A) $8 + 3x = 23; 5$

   (B) $3x - 8 = 23; 5$

   (C) $(8 + 3)x = 23; 2$

   (D) $3x = 8 + 23; 10$

5. Which shows the statement translated into an equation, along with the solution? Seventeen is the difference of a number divided by 2 and 1.

   (A) $17 = \frac{n}{2} - 1; 36$

   (B) $17 = n + \frac{2}{1}; 15$

   (C) $17 = \frac{n}{2} - 1; 9$

   (D) $17 - \frac{n}{2} = 1; 8$

6. Lena wants to buy a computer that costs $900. She already has $473 saved. To help Lena save, her grandmother will pay her $7 an hour to help with yardwork. Which equation can Lena use to determine how many hours, h, she needs to work so that she can buy the computer?

   (A) $\$900 = \$473h + \$7$

   (B) $\$473 = \$7h + \$900$

   (C) $\$900 = \$473 - \$7h$

   (D) $\$900 = \$473 + \$7h$

7. Karen's garden is a rectangle with the dimensions shown. She wants to place a border around its perimeter. Which expression below shows the length of the border she needs?

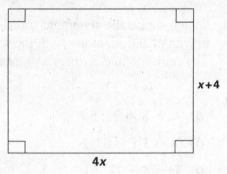

$x+4$

$4x$

Ⓐ $5x + 4$

Ⓑ $10x + 8$

Ⓒ $18x + 8$

Ⓓ $4x^2 \times 16x$

8. Jorge belongs to a science fiction book club that sends 3 books each month. If he started with a collection of 38 books, which equation below can he use to find out how many months it will take to fill his bookshelf, which will hold 64 books?

Ⓐ $64 = 38m + 3$

Ⓑ $64 = 3m + 38$

Ⓒ $3(38) + m = 64$

Ⓓ $3m + 38 = 64$

GPS Practice Pages

M8A1.b

Simplify and evaluate algebraic expressions.

MULTIPLE CHOICE

1. Which shows the expression correctly simplified?
$$3x - 3 - 5x + 3$$

   (A) $8x - 6$

   (B) $8x$

   (C) $-2x - 6$

   (D) $-2x$

2. Which shows the expression correctly simplified?
$$8x + y - 2x - 6y$$

   (A) $10x - 5y$

   (B) $6x - 5y$

   (C) $10x + 7y$

   (D) $6x + 7y$

3. Which shows the polynomial simplified and written in standard form?
$$6g^2 - g - 9 + 4g^2 - g + 4$$

   (A) $2g^2 - 2g - 13$

   (B) $10g^2 - 2g - 5$

   (C) $2g^2 - 13$

   (D) $10g^2 - 5$

4. Which shows the polynomial simplified and written in standard form?
$$-12(x + 2x^2 - 2 - 3x) + 26x^2 - 9$$

   (A) $2x^2 + 50x - 15$

   (B) $2x^2 + 24x + 15$

   (C) $2x^2 - 10x + 15$

   (D) $-2x^2 + 12x + 15$

5. Which shows the expression evaluated for the given value of the variable?
$$9x + 13, x = 8$$

   (A) 72

   (B) 59

   (C) 85

   (D) 30

6. Which shows the expression evaluated for the given values of the variables?
$$a - b + c,$$
   when $a = -3$, $b = -6$, and $c = -5$

   (A) -14

   (B) 8

   (C) -2

   (D) -4

GPS Practice Pages

7. Which shows the expression evaluated for the given values of the variables?

$-y - z$, when $y = 30$ and $z = -35$

Ⓐ 65

Ⓑ −5

Ⓒ −65

Ⓓ 5

8. Which shows the expression evaluated for the given values of the variables?

ab^2, when $a = -3$ and $b = -12$

Ⓐ −1,296

Ⓑ −432

Ⓒ 432

Ⓓ 1,296

M8A1.c
Solve algebraic equations in one variable, including equations involving absolute values.

MULTIPLE CHOICE

1. What is the value of x?
$$-20 = -25 + 5x$$

Ⓐ -9

Ⓑ -6

Ⓒ 1

Ⓓ -4

2. What is the value of r?
$$\frac{r}{4} + 14 = 46$$

Ⓐ 8

Ⓑ 128

Ⓒ 240

Ⓓ $16{,}015$

3. Which value for u is a solution of the equation?
$$18 + 3u = 39$$

Ⓐ 21

Ⓑ 7

Ⓒ 3

Ⓓ 19

4. Which value for n is a solution of the equation?
$$\frac{n}{7} + 47 = 50$$

Ⓐ 679

Ⓑ 21

Ⓒ $\frac{3}{7}$

Ⓓ -21

5. What is the solution to this equation?
$$-2(-6)x = -48$$

Ⓐ -6

Ⓑ -4

Ⓒ 4

Ⓓ 6

6. What is the solution to this equation?
$$\frac{x}{3.9} = 8.7$$

Ⓐ 4.8

Ⓑ 33.93

Ⓒ 122.6

Ⓓ 2.23

GPS Practice Pages

7. What is the value of k in this equation?

$$|-5| \, k + 25 = -15$$

Ⓐ −8

Ⓑ −2

Ⓒ 2

Ⓓ 8

8. Solve the following equation for *x*.

$$-|x| - 8 = 34$$

Ⓐ − 42 only

Ⓑ 42 only

Ⓒ either − 42 or 42

Ⓓ no solution

GPS Practice Pages

M8A1.d
Interpret solutions in problem contexts.

MULTIPLE CHOICE

1. A car travels 21 miles per gallon of gasoline. Which expression below shows the number of miles a car can travel without refilling if it started with g gallons of gas and has already traveled 107 miles?

   Ⓐ $21g + 107$

   Ⓑ $21g - 107$

   Ⓒ $g - 21(107)$

   Ⓓ $g - 107/21$

2. A production worker makes $8.75 per hour plus $0.50 for each part produced. Which expression shows how much the worker makes for producing p parts in an hour?

   Ⓐ $\$8.75p + \$0.50$

   Ⓑ $\$8.75p - \$0.50$

   Ⓒ $\$8.75 - \$0.50p$

   Ⓓ $\$8.75 + \$0.50p$

3. The length of a rectangular yard is 12 feet more than its width. How much fencing is needed to enclose the yard if its length is x feet?

   Ⓐ $4x - 24$

   Ⓑ $4x + 24$

   Ⓒ $4(x - 12)$

   Ⓓ $8x + 24$

4. Shannon charges $12 for each lawn that she mows. If she made $101 in one day, including a $5 tip, which equation can be used to determine the number of lawns that Shannon mowed?

   Ⓐ $101 = 12x - 5$

   Ⓑ $101 = 5x + 12$

   Ⓒ $101 = 12x + 5$

   Ⓓ $101 = 12(x + 5)$

5. The sum of 3 consecutive integers is 72. Which equation can you use to find the value of the smallest of the 3 integers?

   Ⓐ $3y = 72$

   Ⓑ $3y + 3 = 72$

   Ⓒ $3y - 3 = 72$

   Ⓓ $3(y + 1 + 2) = 72$

6. The math club is raising money by having a calendar sale. Jill sold 12 calendars, Peter sold 8 calendars, and Zack sold 14 calendars. If their total sales were $170, how can you calculate the price of each calendar?

   Ⓐ $C = \$170/(12 + 8 + 14)$

   Ⓑ $170C = \$(12 + 8 + 14)$

   Ⓒ $C = \$(12 + 8 + 14)/170$

   Ⓓ $C = \$170 \times (12 + 8 + 14)$

GPS Practice Pages

7. A bank teller counts her $10 and $5 bills at the end of the day. She has a total of 70 bills with a value of $595. Which equation can you use to determine f, the number of $5 bills?

- (A) $595 = f + 10(70 - f)$
- (B) $595 = 5f + 10(70 + f)$
- (C) $70f = 10 + 5(595 - f)$
- (D) $595 = 5f + 10(70 - f)$

8. Ticket for a soccer game cost $6 for adults and $2 for students. Which equation can be used to determine the number of adult tickets sold, a, if there were a total of 435 tickets for $1,370?

- (A) $\$1,370 = \$2a + \$6(435 - a)$
- (B) $\$1,370 = \$6a + \$2(435 - a)$
- (C) $\$1,370 = \$2a + \$6(435 + a)$
- (D) $\$1,370 = \$6a + \$2(435 + a)$

M8A2.a
Represent a given situation using an inequality in one variable.

MULTIPLE CHOICE

1. Pumpkins cost $3.00 or more, depending on size. Which expression shows the cost of 5 pumpkins?

   (A) $\text{Cost} > 5(\$3.00)$

   (B) $\text{Cost} \leq 5(\$3.00)$

   (C) $\text{Cost} \geq 5(\$3.00)$

   (D) $\text{Cost} \geq \dfrac{\$3.00}{5}$

2. If 45 times x is less than 609, which of the following is true?

   (A) $\dfrac{609}{45} \leq x$

   (B) $\dfrac{609}{45} \geq x$

   (C) $\dfrac{609}{45} < x$

   (D) $\dfrac{609}{45} > x$

3. A shipping company will only accept packages for airfreight that weigh less than 90 pounds. Which inequality shows the maximum weight of packing materials that you can ship, if you want to ship two objects weighing 36 pounds and 38.5 pounds in the same package?

   (A) $p \leq 90 - 36 - 38.5$

   (B) $p < 90 - 36 - 38.5$

   (C) $p < 90 + 38.5 - 36$

   (D) $p \geq 36 + 38.5 - 90$

4. To be accepted at a particular college, you must score at least 190 points on an entrance exam that has two sections, English and mathematics. Which inequality shows the score you must have on the English section if your math score is 95?

   (A) $e \geq 190 - 95$

   (B) $e \geq 190 \div 95$

   (C) $e \geq 190 + 95$

   (D) $e \geq \dfrac{190 - 95}{2}$

5. Kishawn is buying two birthday gifts for friends and has $45 to spend. The first gift costs $21.35. Which inequality can be used to determine how much Kishawn can spend on the second gift?

   (A) $x \geq \$45 + \$21.35$

   (B) $x > \$45 - \$21.35$

   (C) $x \leq \$45 + \$21.35$

   (D) $x \leq \$45 - \$21.35$

GPS Practice Pages

6. The maximum load for a large truck is 40,000 pounds. It carries a forklift for loading and unloading that weighs 3,500 pounds. Which inequality below can be used to determine how many 800-pound crates the truck can carry?

Ⓐ $800n + 3{,}500 \geq 40{,}000$

Ⓑ $800n + 3{,}500 < 40{,}000$

Ⓒ $800n + 3{,}500 \leq 40{,}000$

Ⓓ $3{,}500n + 800n \leq 40{,}000$

7. Which inequality can be used to determine the three greatest consecutive integers (x, $x + 1$, and $x + 2$) that have a sum less than 589?

Ⓐ $589 < 3x + 3$

Ⓑ $589 = 3x + 3$

Ⓒ $589 \geq 3x + 3$

Ⓓ $589 > 3x + 3$

8. In order to raise at least $100 for team towels, your swim team decides to sell pizza and subs. The profits are $2.75 for each pizza and $1.45 for each sub. Which inequality can be used to determine how many pizzas you must sell if you sell 48 subs?

Ⓐ $\$100 \geq \$2.75p + 48(\$1.45)$

Ⓑ $\$100 \leq \$2.75p + 48(\$1.45)$

Ⓒ $\$100 \leq \$1.45p + 48(\$2.75)$

Ⓓ $\$100 \leq \$2.75p + \$1.45$

M8A2.b

Use the properties of inequality to solve inequalities.

MULTIPLE CHOICE

1. Solve the inequality. $x - 7 < 4$
   - Ⓐ $x < 11$
   - Ⓑ $x < -3$
   - Ⓒ $x > 11$
   - Ⓓ $x > -3$

2. Solve the inequality. $16 \geq t + 4$
   - Ⓐ $t \geq 12$
   - Ⓑ $12 \leq t$
   - Ⓒ $t \leq 12$
   - Ⓓ $12 > t$

3. Solve the inequality. $\dfrac{m}{3} > -6$
   - Ⓐ $m < -18$
   - Ⓑ $m < 18$
   - Ⓒ $m > -2$
   - Ⓓ $m > -18$

4. Solve the inequality. $5x - 11 \leq 29$
   - Ⓐ $x \leq 8$
   - Ⓑ $x \geq 8$
   - Ⓒ $x \leq \dfrac{18}{5}$
   - Ⓓ $x \leq 200$

5. Solve the inequality. $7x - 12 < 6x - 1$
   - Ⓐ $x > 13$
   - Ⓑ $x < 11$
   - Ⓒ $x < -11$
   - Ⓓ $x < 1$

6. What value of y makes $-\dfrac{1}{2}y > 6$ true?
   - Ⓐ -17.5
   - Ⓑ -9.8
   - Ⓒ 3.2
   - Ⓓ 15.3

GPS Practice Pages

7. Solve the inequality. $-7.1 - w \geq -2.6$

    (A) $w \leq -4.5$

    (B) $w \geq -10.5$

    (C) $w \geq 10.5$

    (D) $w \leq 4.5$

8. Solve the inequality. $-\dfrac{m}{3} > 12$

    (A) $m < 36$

    (B) $m > -36$

    (C) $m < -36$

    (D) $m < -4$

GPS Practice Pages

M8A2.c

Graph the solution of an inequality on a number line.

MULTIPLE CHOICE

1. Which inequality is represented by the graph?

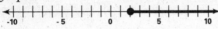

   Ⓐ $m < 2$

   Ⓑ $m \geq 2$

   Ⓒ $m > 2$

   Ⓓ $m \leq 2$

2. Which graph represents the solution to the inequality $11x \geq -22$?

   Ⓐ

   Ⓑ

   Ⓒ

   Ⓓ

3. Which graph represents the solution to the inequality $-1.3x > 9.1$?

   Ⓐ

   Ⓑ

   Ⓒ

   Ⓓ

4. Which graph represents the solution to the inequality $8 + 3x > 14$?

   Ⓐ

   Ⓑ

   Ⓒ

   Ⓓ

5. Which inequality is represented by the graph?

   Ⓐ $2m + 7 \leq 11$

   Ⓑ $m + 7 \geq 11$

   Ⓒ $2m + 7 \geq 11$

   Ⓓ $m + 7 \leq 11$

6. Solve the inequality. Which graph represents its solution?

$$3m + 5 < -4$$

   Ⓐ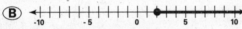

   Ⓑ

   Ⓒ

   Ⓓ

7. Solve the inequality. Which graph represents its solution?

$$4y + 2 \le -34$$

(A) $y \le -9$

```
  <●━━━━┼━━━━━┼━━━━━┼━━━━━┼━>
  -10      -5      0       5      10
```

(B) $y \le -59$

```
  <━━━━━━━━━━━━●━━━━┼━━━━━┼━>
  -69    -64    -59    -54    -49
```

(C) $y \ge -59$

```
  <━━━━┼━━━━━●━━━━━━━━━━━━━━>
  -69    -64    -59    -54    -49
```

(D) $y \le -9$

```
  <●━━━┼━━━━━┼━━━━━┼━━━━━┼━>
  -10      -5      0       5      10
```

8. Solve the inequality. Which graph represents its solution?

$$-7t - 6 \le 22$$

(A) $t \le -4$

```
  <━━━━━━━━━●━━━━┼━━━┼━━━┼━>
   -7  -6  -5  -4  -3  -2  -1   0   1
```

(B) $t \ge 4$

```
  <━━━┼━━━┼━━●━━━━━━━━━━━━━>
   -1   0   1   2   3   4   5   6   7
```

(C) $t \ge -4$

```
  <━━━━━━━━━●━━━━━━━━━━━━━━>
   -7  -6  -5  -4  -3  -2  -1   0   1
```

(D) $t \le 4$

```
  <━━━━━━━━━━━━━━●━━━┼━━━┼━>
   -1   0   1   2   3   4   5   6   7
```

M8A2.d

Interpret solutions in problem contexts.

MULTIPLE CHOICE

1. A tree is 110 inches tall and grows at least 11 inches each year. Which expression describes its height in inches 5 years from now?

   (A) $h \geq 110 - 5(11)$

   (B) $h < 110 + 5(11)$

   (C) $h \leq 110 - 5(11)$

   (D) $h \geq 110 + 5(11)$

2. Yolanda went to the mall and spent $24.53 on a sweater, $6.28 on a pair of socks, and $11.50 on a T-shirt. If she started with $60, what is the maximum she can spend on a pair of jeans?

   (A) $x \leq \$60.00 + \$24.53 + \$6.28 + \$11.50$

   (B) $x \leq \$60.00 - \$24.53 - \$6.28 - \$11.50$

   (C) $x \geq \$60.00 - \$24.53 - \$6.28 - \$11.50$

   (D) $x \geq \$60.00 + \$24.53 + \$6.28 + \$11.50$

3. Your calling card charges $1.25 to place a call and an additional $0.07 for each minute. If the starting balance is $3.00, how many minutes can your call last before the balance reaches $0.00?

   (A) $\$3.00 \leq \$1.25 + \$0.07m$

   (B) $\$3.00 \leq \$1.25m + \$0.07$

   (C) $\$3.00m \leq \$1.25 + \$0.07$

   (D) $\$3.00 \leq \$1.25 - \$0.07m$

4. Mark earns $363 a week. Pedro works for $8.25 an hour. How many hours must Pedro work each week to make more than Mark?

   (A) $h < \$363 \times \$8.25$

   (B) $h \geq \dfrac{\$363}{\$8.25}$

   (C) $h < \dfrac{\$363}{\$8.25}$

   (D) $h > \dfrac{\$363}{\$8.25}$

5. Zack has 18 minutes to walk $\frac{3}{4}$ miles to school. Which inequality shows how fast he must walk, in miles per hour, to be sure that he is not late?

   (A) $s \leq \dfrac{3}{4} \, mile \div \dfrac{18}{60} \, hour$

   (B) $s \leq \dfrac{18}{60} \, hour \div \dfrac{3}{4} \, mile$

   (C) $s \geq \dfrac{3}{4} \, mile \div \dfrac{18}{60} \, hour$

   (D) $s \geq \dfrac{18}{60} \, hour \div \dfrac{3}{4} \, mile$

GPS Practice Pages

6. You are having a pool party and want to order 5 large pizzas. The pizza shop charges $3.75 for delivery. You have $58 to spend. Which inequality can you use to find the most money you can spend on each pizza?

Ⓐ $m \le 5(\$58 - 3.75)$

Ⓑ $m \le \$58 - 5(3.75)$

Ⓒ $m \le \dfrac{\$58 - 3.75}{5}$

Ⓓ $m \le \$58 - 3.75$

7. A kennel owner is buying a new building. He wants each dog run to be at least 96 square feet. The area reserved for the runs is 30 feet by 60 feet. Which inequality can he use to determine how many runs he can install?

Ⓐ $n \le \dfrac{30 \times 60}{96}$

Ⓑ $n \le \dfrac{30 + 60}{96}$

Ⓒ $n \ge \dfrac{30 \times 60}{96}$

Ⓓ $96n \ge 30 \times 60$

8. Your family wants to buy 3 dogs and spend no more than $2,000. Each dog needs a license that costs $15 and a veterinary checkup that costs $100. Which inequality could be used to calculate how much you can spend on each dog?

Ⓐ $3C \le \$2,000 - 300 - 45$

Ⓑ $3C \ge \$2,000 - 300 - 45$

Ⓒ $C \le \$2,000 - 300 - 45$

Ⓓ $C \ge \$2,000 - 300 - 45$

M8A3.a

Recognize a relation as a correspondence between varying quantities.

MULTIPLE CHOICE

1. Which of the following continues this pattern?

$$84, 78, 72, \underline{\quad?\quad}, \underline{\quad?\quad}$$

  Ⓐ 68, 62

  Ⓑ 62, 52

  Ⓒ 66, 60

  Ⓓ 65, 60

2. Which of these patterns can be described by the equation?

$$y = -\frac{1}{2}x$$

  Ⓐ $-\frac{1}{2}, -1, 1\frac{1}{2}, -2 \dots$

  Ⓑ $-1, -2, -3, -4 \dots$

  Ⓒ $-\frac{1}{2}, -\frac{1}{4}, -\frac{1}{8}, -\frac{1}{16} \dots$

  Ⓓ $-\frac{1}{2}, 1, -1\frac{1}{2}, 2, \dots$

3. Which shows the output value for y for an input value of 8 for x?

Input x	2	3	4	5
Output y	6	9	12	15

  Ⓐ 13

  Ⓑ 24

  Ⓒ 18

  Ⓓ 21

4. Which shows the output value for y for an input value of 9 for x?

Input x	1	2	3	4	5
Output y	6	9	12	15	18

  Ⓐ 19

  Ⓑ 21

  Ⓒ 33

  Ⓓ 30

5. What is the value of the dependent variable, if the independent variable is equal to 8?

$$y = 3x + 1$$

  Ⓐ 24

  Ⓑ 25

  Ⓒ 9

  Ⓓ 1

6. What is the value of the dependent variable, if the independent variable is equal to 4?

$$y = -x + 12$$

  Ⓐ 16

  Ⓑ −4

  Ⓒ 12

  Ⓓ 8

GPS Practice Pages

7. Apples cost $0.55 each at the market. Which of these equations describes the relationship between the total cost of a bag of apples and the number of apples, n?

(A) Cost = $0.55n$

(B) Cost = $-($0.55n)$

(C) Cost = $n + 0.55

(D) Cost = $n \div 0.55

8. How would you describe the relation between x and y shown on the graph below?

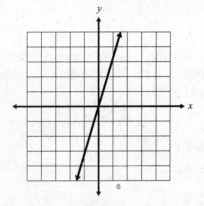

(A) y increases at the same rate as x

(B) y increases one-third as fast as x

(C) y increases three times as fast as x

(D) y and x are not related

M8A3.b

Recognize a function as a correspondence between inputs and outputs where the output for each input must be unique.

MULTIPLE CHOICE

1. Which of the following is a function?

Ⓐ 2, −4, 4, 7

Ⓑ (2, −4), (−4, 7), (2, 7)

Ⓒ (2, −4), (−4, 2), (7, 7)

Ⓓ (2, −4), (4, 7), (4, 2), (7, 4)

2. Which function rule relates x and y?

Input x	1	2	3	4	5
Output y	0	6	12	18	24

Ⓐ $y = -6x + 6$

Ⓑ $y = 6x - 6$

Ⓒ $y = -7x + 7$

Ⓓ $y = 7x + 7$

3. Which function rule relates x and y?

Input x	1	2	3	4	5
Output y	1	−2	−5	−8	−11

Ⓐ $y = 3x + 4$

Ⓑ $y = -3x - 4$

Ⓒ $y = -3x + 4$

Ⓓ $y = -x + 4$

4. Which table of values represents the function rule?

$$y = 4x + 7$$

Ⓐ
Input x	1	2	3	4	5
Output y	−3	1	5	9	13

Ⓑ
Input x	1	2	3	4	5
Output y	11	15	19	23	27

Ⓒ
Input x	1	2	3	4	5
Output y	4	8	12	16	20

Ⓓ
Input x	1	2	3	4	5
Output y	8	9	10	11	12

5. Which value of y completes the function table for the rule $y = 3x^2 - 5$?

Input x	0	2	4	6	8
Output y	−5	7		103	187

Ⓐ 8

Ⓑ 48

Ⓒ 43

Ⓓ 19

6. Which rule describes the linear function that includes the following points?

(1, 5) (3, 9) (5, 13) (7, 17)

Ⓐ $f(x) = 2x + 3$

Ⓑ $f(x) = 3x + 2$

Ⓒ $f(x) = x + 4$

Ⓓ $f(x) = 3x - 4$

GPS Practice Pages

7. Which of the following correctly represents data that is part of the function? $f(x) = 2|x| + 4$

Ⓐ

x	−2	0	2	4	6
f(x)	4	0	4	8	12

Ⓑ

x	−2	0	2	4	6
f(x)	−8	4	8	12	16

Ⓒ

x	8	4	8	12	16
f(x)	−2	0	2	4	6

Ⓓ

x	−2	0	2	4	6
f(x)	8	4	8	12	16

8. Which function rule relates n and A in the arithmetic sequence 15, 11, 7, 3, ...

Ⓐ $A = -n + 7$

Ⓑ $A = -4n + 19$

Ⓒ $A = -6n + 21$

Ⓓ $A = 4n + 19$

GPS Practice Pages

M8A3.c

Distinguish between relations that are functions and those that are not functions.

MULTIPLE CHOICE

1. Determine which relation is a function.

Ⓐ
Input	−1	0	1	2
Output	3	4	3	0

Ⓑ
Input	1	3	1	4
Output	2	1	7	0

Ⓒ
Input	0	1	1	4
Output	2	1	3	0

Ⓓ
Input	2	3	6	2
Output	4	5	−1	0

2. Which of the following relations is a function?

Ⓐ
Input x	Output y
−6	9
−5	7
−5	5

Ⓑ
Input x	Output y
−5	9
−4	7
−5	5

Ⓒ
Input x	Output y
−4	9
−4	7
−5	5

Ⓓ
Input x	Output y
−5	5
−4	2
−3	1

3. Which graph represents a function of *x*?

Ⓐ 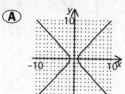 Ⓑ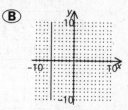

Ⓒ 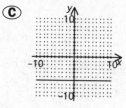 Ⓓ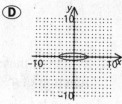

4. Which function is represented by the graph?

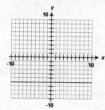

Ⓐ $y = -6$

Ⓑ $x = 6$

Ⓒ $y = 6$

Ⓓ $x = -6$

GPS Practice Pages

5. Which of the following data sets cannot represent a function of x?

(A)

x	-2	0	-2	4	-4
$f(x)$	4	0	4	8	12

(B)

x	-2	0	-2	4	-4
$f(x)$	5	6	7	8	9

(C)

x	-1	0	1	2	3
$f(x)$	4	4	4	4	4

(D)

x	-1	0	1	2	3
$f(x)$	5	6	7	8	9

6. Which of these equations cannot be a function of a?

(A) $b + a = a$

(B) $b = 0$

(C) $b - a = b$

(D) $b = 1/a$

7. Which of these relations does not represent a function?

(A)
```
Input       Output
-3 ────────→ 0
 0 ────────→ 1
 3 ────────→ 2
 6 ────────→ 3
```

(B)
```
Input       Output
-3 ───┐    ┌→ 0
 0 ───┘   ╱  1
 3 ──────╱   2
 6 ─────────→ 3
```

(C)
```
Input       Output
-3 ────────→ 0
 0 ───┐    ┌→ 1
 3 ───┴────→ 2
 6 ────────→ 3
```

(D)
```
Input       Output
-3 ────────→ 0
 0 ──────╲ ╱→ 1
 3 ───────╳  2
 6 ──────╱ ╲  3
```

8. Which of these equations does not represent y as a function of x?

(A) $y = 2x + 1$

(B) $x = 2y + 1$

(C) $y = |x|$

(D) $x = |y|$

GPS Practice Pages

M8A3.d

Recognize functions in a variety of representations and a variety of contexts.

MULTIPLE CHOICE

1. Which is the graph of the function?
$$y = -4x?$$

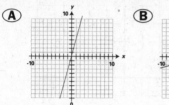
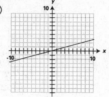

2. Which is the graph of the function?
$$y = \frac{1}{4}x - 3$$

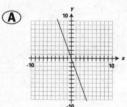
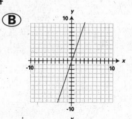
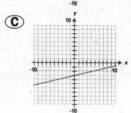
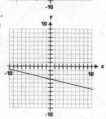

3. Which function rule matches the input-output table?

Input x	−2	−1	0	1	2
Output y	−1	2	5	8	11

   (A) $y = 5x + 3$

   (B) $y = 3x + 5$

   (C) $y = x + 5$

   (D) $y = 3x - 5$

4. Which function rule matches the input-output table?

Input x	−5	−1	0	1	2
Output y	−6.5	−4.5	−4	−3.5	−3.0

   (A) $y = 5x + 3$

   (B) $y = 3x + 5$

   (C) $y = x + 5$

   (D) $y = \frac{1}{2}x - 4$

5. Sara, Rez, and Jonah want to let their friends know about a meeting that same day after school. Each of them contacts two people in 10 minutes, who then contact two different people 10 minutes later, and so on. Which describes the pattern of the number of people called every 10 minutes?

$$3, 6, 12, 24, \ldots$$

   (A) Add three to find the next term.

   (B) Multiply previous term by three to find next term.

   (C) Add six to the find the next term.

   (D) Multiply term by two to find next term.

GPS Practice Pages

6. Which function is represented by the graph?

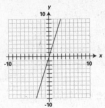

Ⓐ $y = \dfrac{x}{4}$

Ⓑ $y = 4x$

Ⓒ $y = \dfrac{4}{x}$

Ⓓ $y = x + 4$

7. Bobby's Pizzeria cuts a 6" pie into two pieces, an 8" pie into 4 pieces, and a 10" pie into six pieces. If this pattern continues, how many pieces will a 14" pizza be cut into?

Ⓐ 8

Ⓑ 10

Ⓒ 12

Ⓓ 20

8. Which function below describes the data shown on the graph?

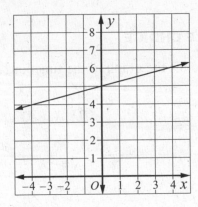

Ⓐ $y = \dfrac{x}{4} - 5$

Ⓑ $y = 4x + 5$

Ⓒ $y = \dfrac{x}{4} + 5$

Ⓓ $y = 5 - \dfrac{x}{4}$

GPS Practice Pages

M8A3.e

Use tables to describe sequences recursively and with a formula in closed form.

MULTIPLE CHOICE

1. Which table shows a set of values for the equation?

$$12x - 3y = -21$$

Ⓐ
x	-2	-1	0	1	2
y	0	4	8	12	16

Ⓑ
x	-2	-1	0	1	2
y	-16	-12	-8	-4	0

Ⓒ
x	-2	-1	0	1	2
y	-15	-11	-7	-3	1

Ⓓ
x	-2	-1	0	1	2
y	-1	3	7	11	15

2. Which equation in two variables represents the values in the table?

x	-2	-1	0	1
y	7	5	3	1

Ⓐ $-4x - 2y = -6$

Ⓑ $-10x - 5y = -15$

Ⓒ $-40x - 20y = -60$

Ⓓ all of these

3. Which completes the table of values for the equation?

$$-3x - y = 15$$

x	-2	-1	0	1	2
y					

Ⓐ $-9, -12, -15, -18, -21$

Ⓑ $9, 12, 15, 18, 21$

Ⓒ $-9, -6, -3, 0, 3$

Ⓓ none of these

4. Garden soil can be purchased for $9.00 per cubic yard, with a $20.00 delivery fee. This situation can be modeled by the equation $y = 9x + 20$. Make a table of values for the equation.

Ⓐ
Input x	1	2	3	4	5
Output y	11	2	-7	-16	-25

Ⓑ
Input x	1	2	3	4	5
Output y	29	30	31	32	33

Ⓒ
Input x	1	2	3	4	5
Output y	29	38	47	56	65

Ⓓ
Input x	1	2	3	4	5
Output y	21	22	23	24	25

5. Which completes the table of values for the equation?

$$y = 4x - 9$$

Input x	1	2	3	4	5
Output y					

Ⓐ $-5, -9, -13, -17, -21$

Ⓑ $13, 17, 21, 25, 29$

Ⓒ $-5, -1, 3, 7, 11$

Ⓓ none of these

GPS Practice Pages

6. Which completes the table of values for the equation?

$$y = -\frac{1}{2}x + 3$$

Input x	1	2	3	4	5
Output y					

(A) $-2\frac{1}{2}, -2, -1\frac{1}{2}, -1, -\frac{1}{2}$

(B) $2\frac{1}{2}, 2, 1\frac{1}{2}, 1, \frac{1}{2}$

(C) $3\frac{1}{2}, 4, 4\frac{1}{2}, 5, 5\frac{1}{2}$

(D) none of these

7. Which rule is represented by the input-output table?

Input x	0	1	2	3	4
Output y	6	9	12	15	18

(A) $y = 3x + 6$

(B) $y = 3x^2 + 6$

(C) $y = x + 6$

(D) $y = -3x - 6$

8. Which rule is represented by the input-output table?

Input x	0	1	2	3	4
Output y	7	6	5	4	3

(A) $y = x + 7$

(B) $y = x^2 + 7$

(C) $y = x - 7$

(D) $y = -x + 7$

M8A3.f

Understand and recognize arithmetic sequences as linear functions with whole number input values.

MULTIPLE CHOICE

1. Which shows the first five numbers of the following pattern?
   Start with 4 and add 6 repeatedly.

   (A) 4, 16, 22, 28, 34

   (B) 4, 24, 48, 72, 96

   (C) 4, 10, 16, 22, 28

   (D) 6, 10, 14, 18, 22

2. Which describes the pattern?
   5, 20, 80, 320 ...

   (A) Start with 5 and add 4 repeatedly.

   (B) Start with 5 and multiply by 4 repeatedly.

   (C) Start with 5 and add 20 repeatedly.

   (D) Start with 4 and multiply by 5 repeatedly.

3. Which describes the pattern and shows the next three numbers?
   5, 8, 11, 14 ...

   (A) Add 3 to the number;
   17, 21, 25

   (B) Multiply the number by 2;
   28, 56, 112

   (C) Add 3 to the number;
   17, 20, 23

   (D) Subtract 3 from the number;
   11, 8, 5

4. Which describes the pattern and shows the next three numbers?
   5, 11, 23, 47 ...

   (A) Add 6 to the number;
   53, 59, 65

   (B) Multiply the number by 2;
   94, 188, 376

   (C) Multiply the number by 2, add 1;
   95, 191, 382

   (D) Add 2 to the number, multiply by 3;
   98, 200, 404

5. Which function rule matches the input-output table?

Input x	1	2	3	4	5
Output y	−5	0	5	10	15

   (A) $y = -11 + 6x$

   (B) $y = 6 - 11x$

   (C) $y = -10 + 5x$

   (D) $y = 5 - 10x$

6. Mark bicycles at a rate of 12 miles per hour. Which completes the table?

Hours	1	2	3	4	5
Miles	12	24	36		

   (A) 48, 70

   (B) 48, 60

   (C) 58, 70

   (D) 40, 45

7. Which describes the pattern and shows the next three numbers?
4,096, 1,024, 256, 64 ...

(A) Subtract 3,072 from the number;
$-3,008, -6,080, -9,152$

(B) Divide the number by 4;
16, 4, 1

(C) Multiply the number by 4;
256, 1,024, 4,096

(D) Divide the number by 16;
$4, \frac{1}{4}, \frac{1}{64}$

8. Which function rule matches the input-output table?

Input x	0	1	2	3	4
Output y	−3	0	3	6	9

(A) $y = 3x + 3$

(B) $y = 3x$

(C) $y = x - 3$

(D) $y = 3x - 3$

M8A3.g

Interpret the constant difference in an arithmetic sequence as the slope of the associated linear function.

MULTIPLE CHOICE

1. The *y*-axis of the graph represents the speed at which a cyclist bikes in miles per hour. The *x*-axis represents the time in seconds passed. Which statement is true?

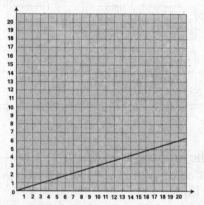

ⓐ The cyclist's speed increases steadily over time.

ⓑ The speed of the cyclist decreases over time.

ⓒ The speed of the cyclist is a constant over time.

ⓓ The cyclist had stopped and is increasing his speed at a constant rate after starting.

2. Which shows an input-output table and the range for the function $y = -2.5x$ using the domain $-2, -1, 0, 1,$ and 2?

ⓐ
Input x	−2	−1	0	1	2
Output y	−5	−2.5	0	2.5	5

Range: $-5, -2.5, 0, 2.5, 5$

ⓑ
Input x	−2	−1	0	1	2
Output y	5	2.5	0	−2.5	−5

Range: $-2, -1, 0, 1, 2$

ⓒ
Input x	−2	−1	0	1	2
Output y	−5	−2.5	0	2.5	5

Range: $-2, -1, 0, 1, 2$

ⓓ
Input x	−2	−1	0	1	2
Output y	5	2.5	0	−2.5	−5

Range: $-5, -2.5, 0, 2.5, 5$

3. Which shows the rule for the function table?

Input x	2	3	4	5
Output y	6	9	12	15

ⓐ $y = x + 4$

ⓑ $y = x - 2$

ⓒ $y = \dfrac{3}{x}$

ⓓ $y = 3x$

GPS Practice Pages

4. Which shows the rule for the function table?

Input x	−2	−1	0	1
Output y	−1	−0.5	0	0.5

(A) $y = -\frac{1}{2}x$

(B) $y = \frac{1}{2}x$

(C) $y = x + \frac{1}{2}$

(D) $y = \frac{1}{2}x - \frac{1}{2}$

5. Write a function rule for the pattern. Each figure in the pattern is made using unit squares. The input x is the number below each figure, and the output y is the number of unit squares in the figure.

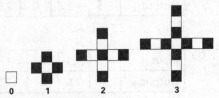

(A) $y = 4x$

(B) $y = x + 4$

(C) $y = 4x + 1$

(D) $y = x^2 + 1$

6. If the arithmetic sequence below is plotted on a graph, what is the slope of the line?

44, 56, 68, 80, ...

(A) $\frac{1}{12}$

(B) 12

(C) 32

(D) 44

7. Which of these tables shows a linear function that has a slope of 3?

(A)

x	−2	0	2	4	6
f(x)	−5	1	7	13	19

(B)

x	−2	0	2	4	6
f(x)	−5	−2	1	4	7

(C)

x	−2	0	2	4	6
f(x)	$\frac{1}{3}$	$\frac{2}{3}$	1	$1\frac{1}{3}$	$1\frac{2}{3}$

(D)

x	−2	0	2	4	6
f(x)	$\frac{2}{3}$	$1\frac{1}{3}$	7	$2\frac{2}{3}$	$3\frac{1}{3}$

8. If the arithmetic sequence below is plotted on a graph, what is the slope of the line?

−0.08, −0.13, −0.18, −0.23, ...

(A) −20

(B) −0.05

(C) −0.5

(D) 2

M8A3.h
Identify relations and functions as linear or nonlinear.

MULTIPLE CHOICE

1. Which of the following pairs of coordinates are included on a line defined by a linear function?

   Ⓐ (0, 1), (1, 3), (2, 8), (3, 15)

   Ⓑ (0, 1), (1, 3), (2, 5), (3, 7)

   Ⓒ (0, 1), (1, −3), (2, 5), (3, −7)

   Ⓓ (0, 1), (1, −3), (2, −10), (3, −25)

2. Which of the following pairs of coordinates does not describe a linear function?

   Ⓐ (1, 5), (2, 10), (3, 15), (4, 20)

   Ⓑ (1, −5), (2, −10), (3, −15), (4, −20)

   Ⓒ (1, 5), (2, 8), (3, 12), (4, 17)

   Ⓓ (1, 5), (2, 8), (3, 11), (4, 14)

3. Which of these equations represents a linear function?

   Ⓐ $y = \dfrac{x^2}{2}$

   Ⓑ $y = \dfrac{x^2}{x} + 9$

   Ⓒ $y = x(14 - 3x) + 2$

   Ⓓ $y = \dfrac{x^2 + 9}{x}$

4. Which of these tables does not represent a linear function?

   Ⓐ
x	−3	−2	−1	0	1	2
f(x)	−5	−3	−1	1	3	5

   Ⓑ
x	−3	−2	−1	0	1	2
f(x)	100	92	84	76	68	60

   Ⓒ
x	−3	−2	−1	0	1	2
f(x)	0.2	0.35	0.5	0.65	0.8	0.95

   Ⓓ
x	−3	−2	−1	0	1	2
f(x)	6	4	2	0	2	4

5. Which function is not linear?

   Ⓐ $y = \dfrac{x}{2}x + \dfrac{15}{11}$

   Ⓑ $y - \dfrac{x}{8} = 26$

   Ⓒ $y = \dfrac{x + 5}{3}$

   Ⓓ $y = \dfrac{6}{x} + 33$

GPS Practice Pages

6. Which graph represents a linear function?

Ⓐ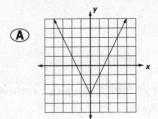

Ⓑ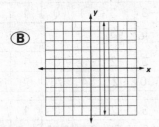

Ⓒ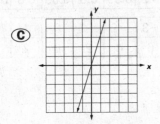

Ⓓ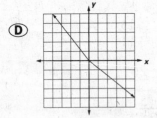

7. Which function is not linear?

Ⓐ $y = 7\left(\dfrac{x}{5} - 18\right)$

Ⓑ $y = 7\left(\dfrac{x - 18}{5}\right)$

Ⓒ $y = 7x\left(\dfrac{x}{5} - 18\right)$

Ⓓ $y = \dfrac{7x}{5} - 18$

8. Which of these tables represents a linear function?

Ⓐ

x	0	2	5	10	15	20
f(x)	−14	−12	−9	−4	1	6

Ⓑ

x	0	2	5	10	15	20
f(x)	5	10	15	20	25	30

Ⓒ

x	0	2	5	10	15	20
f(x)	10	12	18	26	38	52

Ⓓ

x	0	2	5	10	15	20
f(x)	5	7	10	14	19	25

GPS Practice Pages

M8A3.i
Translate among verbal, tabular, graphic, and algebraic representations of functions.

MULTIPLE CHOICE

1. Jeffrey uses 28 nails to build a picture frame. Which completes the table?

Picture frame	1	2	3	4	5
Nails	28	56	84		

  Ⓐ 140, 168   Ⓑ 112, 140

  Ⓒ 88, 93   Ⓓ 102, 130

2. There are 16 pastries per carton. Which completes the table?

Carton	1	2	3	4	5
Pastries	16	32	48		

  Ⓐ 80, 96   Ⓑ 54, 70

  Ⓒ 52, 57   Ⓓ 64, 80

3. An artist displays wall hangings of different sizes, as shown below. Which shows the next wall hanging in the pattern?

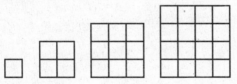

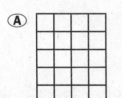 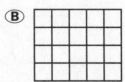

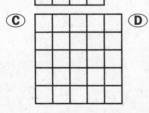 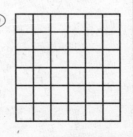

4. What is the total cost of a phone call that lasts 20 minutes, according to the graph?

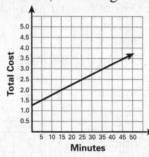

  Ⓐ $1.00

  Ⓑ $1.25

  Ⓒ $2.25

  Ⓓ $3.25

5. Which is the graph of the function?
$$y = 4x$$

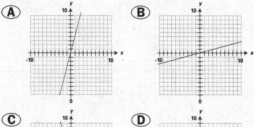

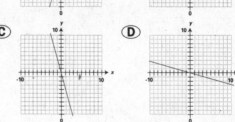

GPS Practice Pages

6. A tomato plant in Anna's garden was 8 centimeters tall when it was first planted. Since then, it has grown approximately 1.3 centimeters per day. Which table expresses the tomato plant's height, *H*, in terms of the number of days, *d*, since it was planted?

Ⓐ
Input d	1	2	3	4	5
Output h	1.3	2.6	3.9	5.2	6.5

Ⓑ
Input d	1	2	3	4	5
Output h	9.3	10.6	11.9	13.2	14.5

Ⓒ
Input d	1	2	3	4	5
Output h	6.7	5.4	4.1	2.8	1.5

Ⓓ
Input d	1	2	3	4	5
Output h	6.7	8	9.3	10.6	11.9

7. Which shows a graph of the linear equation?

$$y = -\frac{1}{4}x - 3$$

Ⓐ 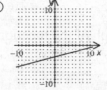   Ⓑ

Ⓒ 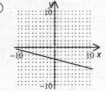   Ⓓ

8. Which shows a graph of the linear equation?

$$y = 3$$

Ⓐ 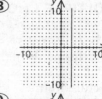   Ⓑ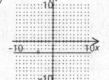

Ⓒ 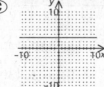   Ⓓ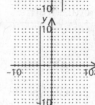

GPS Practice Pages

M8A4.a

Interpret slope as a rate of change.

MULTIPLE CHOICE

1. Which shows the slope of the line?

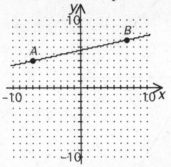

A $-\dfrac{3}{14}$ **B** $-\dfrac{14}{3}$

C $\dfrac{14}{3}$ **D** $\dfrac{3}{14}$

2. The *y*-axis of the graph represents the length of a balloon in inches. The *x*-axis represents the time in days passed. Which statement is true?

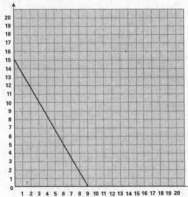

A The rate at which the size of the balloon decreases gets faster each day.

B The rate at which the size of the balloon increases remains constant.

C The rate at which the size of the balloon increases gets slower each day.

D The rate at which the size of the balloon decreases remains constant.

3. The *y*-axis of the graph represents the speed at which an escalator moves in miles per hour. The *x*-axis represents the time in minutes passed. Which statement is true?

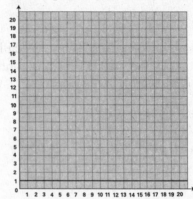

A The speed of the escalator increases over time.

B The speed of the escalator decreases over time.

C The speed of the escalator is a constant over time.

D The escalator is stopped.

4. A business makes regular deposits into a savings account at the rate of $1,850 per week. Which table expresses the account's balance, *m*, in terms of the number of weeks, *w*, that have passed?

A

Input *w*	1	2	3	4	5
Output *m*	$0	$1,850	$3,700	$5,550	$9,250

B

Input *w*	1	2	3	4	5
Output *m*	$12,950	$25,900	$38,850	$51,800	$64,750

C

Input *w*	1	2	3	4	5
Output *m*	$1,850	$3,700	$5,550	$7,400	$9,250

D

Input *w*	1	2	3	4	5
Output *m*	$3,700	$5,550	$7,400	$9,250	$11,100

5. Find the slope of the line passing through the points.

$$(-9, -3), (-4, -2)$$

- Ⓐ $\frac{1}{5}$
- Ⓑ $\frac{1}{3}$
- Ⓒ 5
- Ⓓ 3

6. A mountain road rises 2 feet vertically for every 18 feet that it runs horizontally. What is the slope of the road?

- Ⓐ $\frac{1}{9}$
- Ⓑ $\frac{1}{2}$
- Ⓒ 9
- Ⓓ 36

7. A waterslide has a slope of $\frac{4}{3}$. Which of the diagrams below best represents the appearance of the waterslide as viewed from one side?

Ⓐ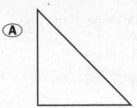

Ⓑ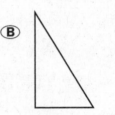

Ⓒ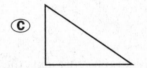

Ⓓ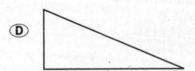

8. A diver comes up from a deep dive slowly to avoid decompression sickness. The table below shows one diver's depth over time. If the change in depth were graphed with time on the *x*-axis and depth on the *y*-axis, what is the slope of the line?

Time (min.)	4	8	12	16
Depth (ft.)	160	140	120	100

- Ⓐ −20 ft./min.
- Ⓑ −5 ft./min.
- Ⓒ 0.2 ft./min.
- Ⓓ 5 ft./min.

M8A4.b

Determine the meaning of the slope and *y*-intercept in a given situation.

MULTIPLE CHOICE

1. You are selling magazine subscriptions to raise $230 to pay for summer camp. As shown on the graph, you already have $180. Use the slope of the line to determine how many more subscriptions you need to sell to have enough money.

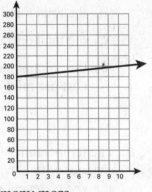

Ⓐ 25 subscriptions

Ⓑ 24 subscriptions

Ⓒ 50 subscriptions

Ⓓ 2 subscriptions

2. Jasmine went to the Funland Amusement Park on Tuesday. Of her $28, she spent $4 on food. Use the slope of the line to determine the number of ride tickets she was able to buy with the rest of her money.

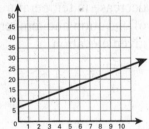

Ⓐ 9 rides

Ⓑ 12 rides

Ⓒ 21 rides

Ⓓ 16 rides

3. Which graph shows the line with the given intercepts?

x-intercept: −3, *y*-intercept: −5

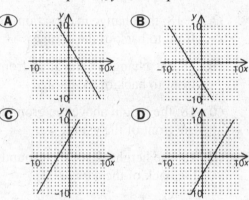

4. Identify the slope and the *y*-intercept of the equation.

$$y = 0.034x + 0.665$$

Ⓐ slope = 0.034;
y-intercept = (0, 0.665)

Ⓑ slope = 0.034;
y-intercept = (0.665, 0)

Ⓒ slope = 0.034;
y-intercept = (0, 0.034)

Ⓓ slope = −0.034;
y-intercept = (0, 0.665)

GPS Practice Pages

5. A second-level deck in a parking garage increases in elevation by 1 foot for every 15 feet horizontally. The elevation above the ground at any particular point is:

$$E = \frac{1}{15}d + 18$$

where E is the elevation and d is the horizontal distance from the front of the garage. What is the y-intercept of this equation and what does it represent?

Ⓐ -18; the change in elevation from front to back of the garage

Ⓑ 18; the change in elevation from front to back of the garage

Ⓒ 18; the height above the ground at the front of the garage

Ⓓ 18; the height above the ground at the back of the garage

6. Mark adds $25 to his savings account every month, starting with $300. He can calculate his current savings using the formula:

Balance = 25m + 300

where m represents the number of months. What are the slope and y-intercept of this equation?

Ⓐ Slope $= -25$;
y-intercept $= 300$

Ⓑ Slope $= 25$;
y-intercept $= 300/25 = 12$

Ⓒ Slope $= 25$;
y-intercept $= 25/300 = \frac{1}{12}$

Ⓓ Slope $= 25$;
y-intercept $= 300$

7. The equation for the cost of a one-day car rental is shown below. What does the y-intercept of this equation represent?

$Cost = (\$0.45)(miles\ driven) + \$23.00$

Ⓐ the cost per mile driven

Ⓑ the total number of miles driven

Ⓒ the total cost of the rental

Ⓓ the amount paid in addition to the cost per mile

8. The temperature on a mountain trail changes with elevation. The temperature at a given elevation above the base of the mountain can be calculated using the equation below, where T is the temperature and h is the elevation in feet above the beginning of the trail. What do the slope and y-intercept of this equation represent?

$$T = -0.005°Fh + 50.9°F$$

Ⓐ increase in temperature per foot of elevation and temperature at the base

Ⓑ decrease in temperature per foot of elevation and temperature at the base

Ⓒ increase in temperature per foot of elevation and temperature at the given elevation

Ⓓ decrease in temperature per foot of elevation and temperature at the given elevation

GPS Practice Pages

M8A4.c

Graph equations of the form $y = mx + b$.

MULTIPLE CHOICE

1. Which graph represents the equation?
$$y = \frac{1}{3}x - 1$$

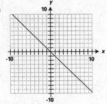 Ⓐ
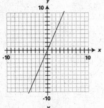 Ⓑ

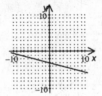 Ⓒ
 Ⓓ

2. Which shows a graph of the linear equation?
$$y = -\frac{1}{4}x + 3$$

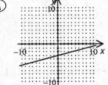 Ⓐ
 Ⓑ

Ⓒ   Ⓓ

3. Which shows a graph of the linear equation?
$$y = -3$$

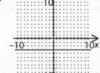 Ⓐ
 Ⓑ

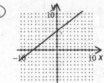 Ⓒ
 Ⓓ

4. Which shows a graph of the linear equation?
$$y = -\frac{3}{4}x - 5$$

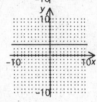 Ⓐ
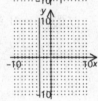 Ⓑ

 Ⓒ
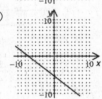 Ⓓ

5. Which equation describes this graph?

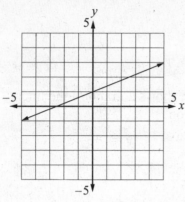

Ⓐ $y = 2.5x + 1$

Ⓑ $y = 2.5x - 1$

Ⓒ $y = 0.2x + 1$

Ⓓ $y = -2.5x + 1$

6. Which equation describes this graph?

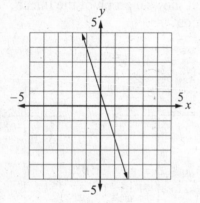

Ⓐ $y = -\dfrac{1}{2}x + 1$

Ⓑ $y = -\dfrac{1}{3}x + 1$

Ⓒ $y = -3x + 1$

Ⓓ $y = \dfrac{1}{3}x + 1$

7. Which graph plots the function?
$y = -2x - 2$

Ⓐ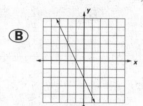

Ⓑ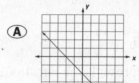

Ⓒ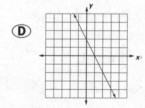

Ⓓ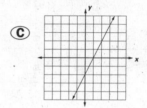

8. What is the slope-intercept equation of this graph?

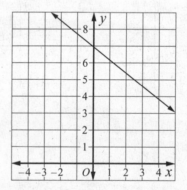

Ⓐ $y = -\dfrac{4}{3}x + 7$

Ⓑ $y = -x + 7$

Ⓒ $y = \dfrac{4}{3}x - 7$

Ⓓ $y = -\dfrac{3}{4}x + 7$

GPS Practice Pages

M8A4.d

Graph equations of the form $ax + by = c$.

MULTIPLE CHOICE

1. Which is the graph of the function?
$$y = 0.25x - 3$$

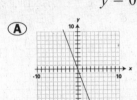

Ⓐ 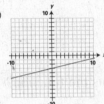 Ⓑ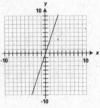

Ⓒ 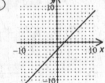 Ⓓ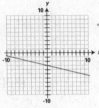

2. Which shows a graph of the linear equation?
$$x + y = 2$$

Ⓐ 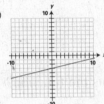 Ⓑ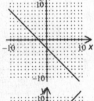

Ⓒ 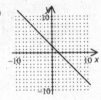 Ⓓ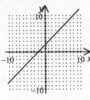

3. Which equation is represented by the graph?

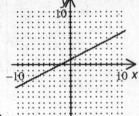
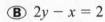
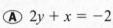

Ⓐ $2y + x = -2$

Ⓑ $2y - x = 2$

Ⓒ $-2y + x = -2$

Ⓓ $-2y - x = -2$

4. Which equation describes this graph?

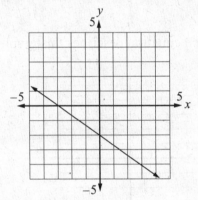

Ⓐ $-2x + 3y = 0$

Ⓑ $3y + 2x = -6$

Ⓒ $2x + 3y = 0$

Ⓓ $2x + 3y = 6$

GPS Practice Pages

5. Which equation describes this graph?

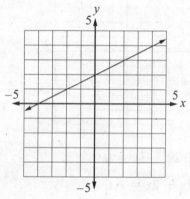

(A) $3x + 3y = 6$

(B) $2x - 3y = 6$

(C) $2x + 3y = 0$

(D) $2x + 3y = 6$

6. Which equation describes this graph?

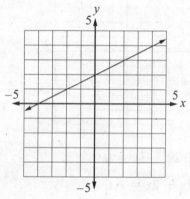

(A) $-2x + y = 0$

(B) $-x + 2y = 4$

(C) $-2x + y = 4$

(D) $x + 2y = 4$

7. Which graph plots the function?
$$3x + 4y = 12$$

(A) 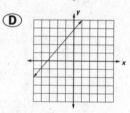 (B)

(C) 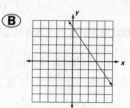 (D)

8. Which graph plots the function?
$$1\frac{1}{2}x - 3y = 3$$

(A) 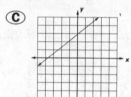 (B)

(C) 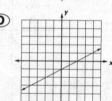 (D)

M8A4.e

Determine the equation of a line given a graph, numerical information that defines the line, or a context involving a linear relationship.

MULTIPLE CHOICE

1. A truck is traveling at a constant speed of 50 miles per hour toward Atlanta. At the beginning of the trip, the truck is 368 miles from the city. Which equation can be used to determine its distance at a time, t, in hours from the beginning of the trip?

   A $d = 368 + 50t$

   B $d = 368 - 50t$

   C $d = 50t - 368$

   D $d = 368t - 50$

2. Which shows the equation of the graph in slope-intercept form?

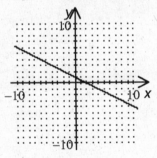

   A $y = -2x + 1$

   B $y = -\frac{1}{2}x - 1$

   C $y = \frac{1}{2}x - 1$

   D $y = -\frac{1}{2}x + 1$

3. Which equation is represented by the graph?

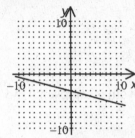

   A $y = -\frac{1}{4}x - 3$

   B $y = \frac{1}{4}x - 3$

   C $y = -\frac{1}{4}x + 3$

   D $-y = -\frac{1}{4}x - 3$

4. Which equation is represented by the graph?

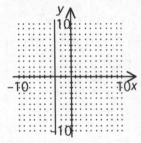

   A $y = -3$

   B $x = 3$

   C $y = x - 3$

   D $x = -3$

GPS Practice Pages

5. Which function rule relates x and y?

Input x	1	2	3	4	5
Output y	-12	-15	-18	-21	-24

(A) $y = -3x + 9$

(B) $y = -3x - 9$

(C) $y = 9x - 3$

(D) $y = 3x - 9$

6. Which table of values represents the function rule?
$$3x + y = 9$$

(A)

Input x	-2	-1	0	1
Output y	15	12	9	6

(B)

Input x	-2	-1	0	1
Output y	-15	-12	-9	-6

(C)

Input x	-2	-1	0	1
Output y	9	9	9	9

(D)

Input x	-2	-1	0	4
Output y	14	13	8	5

7. Which table of values represents the function rule?
$$-2x + y = 8$$

(A)

Input x	1	2	3	4	5
Output y	6	4	2	0	-2

(B)

Input x	1	2	3	4	5
Output y	10	8	6	4	2

(C)

Input x	1	2	3	4	5
Output y	10	12	14	16	18

(D)

Input x	1	2	3	4	5
Output y	10	14	18	22	26

8. Which shows the equation of the graph in slope-intercept form?

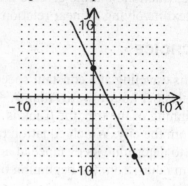

(A) $y = x + 4$

(B) $y = 2x + 4$

(C) $y = -x + 4$

(D) $y = -2x + 4$

GPS Practice Pages

M8A4.f
Solve problems involving linear relationships.

MULTIPLE CHOICE

1. The cost of a school banquet is $95 plus $13 for each person attending. What is the cost for 75 people?

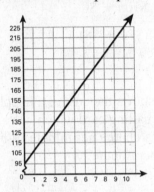

  Ⓐ $950

  Ⓑ $1,070

  Ⓒ $1,145

  Ⓓ $1,350

2. Garden soil can be purchased for $7.00 per cubic yard, with a $24.00 delivery fee. How much will 8 cubic yards of soil cost?

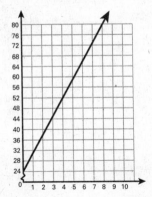

  Ⓐ $80

  Ⓑ $56

  Ⓒ $52

  Ⓓ $248

3. Kelly wants to buy a stereo that costs $400. She already has $127 saved. Her job pays her $11 an hour. How many hours will Kelly need to work before she can afford to buy the stereo?

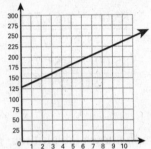

  Ⓐ 273 hours

  Ⓑ 24 hours

  Ⓒ 25 hours

  Ⓓ 37 hours

4. The front wheel of a child's riding toy travels $2\frac{1}{2}$ feet for every rotation it makes. Which function and graph models the distance, y, the front wheel travels in x rotations?

  Ⓐ $y = 2\frac{1}{2}x$ Ⓑ $y = 2\frac{1}{2}x$

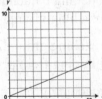 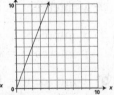

  Ⓒ $y = \frac{2}{5}x$ Ⓓ $y = \frac{2}{5}x$

 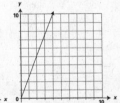

GPS Practice Pages

5. Several friends went to a buffet dinner that costs $15.95 per person. Three people also ordered a beverage that cost $1.75. If the total bill was $85.00, which equation below could be used to determine the number of diners?

(A) $x = \dfrac{\$85.00}{\$15.95 - 3(\$1.75)}$

(B) $x = \dfrac{\$85.00 - \$15.95}{3(\$1.75)}$

(C) $x = \dfrac{\$85.00 - 3(\$1.75)}{\$15.95}$

(D) $x = \dfrac{\$85.00 + 3(\$1.75)}{\$15.95}$

6. This graph shows the altitude, y, in feet of a parachutist x seconds after opening the parachute. What do the x- and y-intercepts of this graph represent?

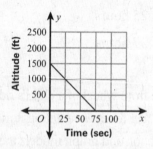

(A) x-intercept = jumping from plane; y-intercept = reaching ground

(B) x-intercept = opening parachute; y-intercept = reaching ground

(C) x-intercept = reaching ground; y-intercept = jumping from plane

(D) x-intercept = reaching ground; y-intercept = opening parachute

7. Renting a canoe costs $8.00 per hour and a return trip to your starting point costs $10.00. Which equation could you use to calculate the cost of a canoe trip that lasts h hours?

(A) Cost = $8h − $10

(B) Cost = $8h + $10

(C) Cost = $10h + $8

(D) Cost = ($10 + $8)

8. This graph shows the cost of a telephone call using a calling card which has a fixed charge plus a charge per minute. What is the charge per minute?

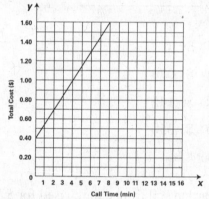

(A) $0.15

(B) $0.30

(C) $0.55

(D) $1.50

GPS Practice Pages

M8A5.a

Given a problem context, write an appropriate system of linear equations.

MULTIPLE CHOICE

1. A business needs to decide whether to rent or buy a copy machine. The rental is $200 per year plus 8 cents per copy. To buy the machine costs $1,200 but the supplies only cost 4 cents per copy. Which set of linear equations can be used to determine the number of copies needed to make the costs equal?

   Ⓐ $y = \$200x + \$0.08$
   $y = \$1,200x + \$0.04$

   Ⓑ $y = \$200 + \$0.04x$
   $y = \$1,200 - \$0.08x$

   Ⓒ $y = \$200 + \$0.08x$
   $y = \$1,200 + \$0.04x$

   Ⓓ $y = \$200 + \$0.08y$
   $x = \$1,200 + \$0.04x$

2. A store display has room for 96 different canned goods. The manager wants to display half as many canned fruits as canned vegetables. Which set of linear equations can he use to determine the number of each type of canned goods to display?

   Ⓐ $f + v = 96$
   $f - 0.5v = 0$

   Ⓑ $f + v = 96$
   $v - 0.5f = 0$

   Ⓒ $f = v + 96$
   $f - 0.5v = 0$

   Ⓓ $2f + v = 96$
   $f + 2v = 0$

3. Ralph bought two packs of baseball cards and four graphic novels for $20. Jamie bought one pack of baseball cards and six comic books, which cost $25. Which system of linear equations can be used to calculate the cost of a pack of baseball cards (*b*) and the cost of a graphic novel (*n*)?

   Ⓐ $4n + 6n = 25$
   $2b + b = 20$

   Ⓑ $b + 4n = 25$
   $2b + 6n = 20$

   Ⓒ $6b + n = 25$
   $2b + 4n = 20$

   Ⓓ $b + 6n = 25$
   $2b + 4n = 20$

4. Lisa plans to spend 5 hours over the weekend on homework projects. She has two projects and she wants to spend 3 times as much of her work time on a reading assignment as she spends on math review. Which system of equations can she use to calculate the amount of time to assign to each project?

   Ⓐ $r - m = 5$
   $r = 3m$

   Ⓑ $r + m = 5$
   $r = 3m$

   Ⓒ $r + 3m = 5$
   $r = 3m$

   Ⓓ $3r + m = 5$
   $r = m$

GPS Practice Pages

5. A movie had ticket sales of 34 million dollars in its first two weeks of release. The second week the sales dropped by $\frac{1}{3}$ compared to the first week. Which system of equations can be used to calculate the sales in the first week, a, and the sales in the second week, b?

Ⓐ $a + \$34,000,000 = b$
   $b = \frac{2}{3}a$

Ⓑ $a + b = \$34,000,000$
   $b = \frac{1}{3}a$

Ⓒ $a + b = \$34,000,000$
   $b = \frac{2}{3}a$

Ⓓ $a + b = \$34,000,000$
   $b + \frac{2}{3}a = 0$

6. Lee bought 2 CDs and a book for $35. Marcy bought 6 books and 1 CD for $79. If the prices for all the CDs and all the books were the same, which system of linear equations can be used to calculate the prices?

Ⓐ $b - 2c = \$35$
   $6b - c = \$79$

Ⓑ $b + c = \$35$
   $6b + c = \$79$

Ⓒ $b = \$35 + 2c$
   $6b = \$79 + c$

Ⓓ $b = \$35 - 2c$
   $6b = \$79 - c$

7. A new business had $20,000 in start-up costs for the store with $500 per day in operating costs. The store makes $1,200 each day. How many days (x) will it take for the store to cover its costs?

Ⓐ $y = \$500x + \$20,000$
   $y = \$1,200x$

Ⓑ $y = \$1,200x$
   $y = \$1,200x + \$20,000$

Ⓒ $y = \$500x - \$20,000$
   $y = \$1,200x$

Ⓓ $y = \$500x + \$1,200$
   $y = \$20,000x$

8. Carl mailed 50 letters and post cards at the post office. A letter stamp costs 39 cents and a post card stamp costs 25 cents. If Carl spent $16.70 for postage, which set of equations can be used to calculate how many letters and how many post cards he sent?

Ⓐ $l + c = 50$
   $\$0.39l + \$0.25c + \$16.70 = 0$

Ⓑ $l + c + 50 = 0$
   $\$0.39l + \$0.25c = \$16.70$

Ⓒ $l - c = 50$
   $\$0.39l - \$0.25c = \$16.70$

Ⓓ $l + c = 50$
   $\$0.39l + \$0.25c = \$16.70$

GPS Practice Pages

M8A5.b

Solve systems of equations graphically and algebraically, using technology as appropriate.

MULTIPLE CHOICE

1. What is the solution to the system of linear equations?

$$y + x = 3$$
$$y - x = 1$$

Ⓐ $(-1, 4)$

Ⓑ $(1, 2)$

Ⓒ $(2, 1)$

Ⓓ $(3, 0)$

2. What is the solution to the system of linear equations?

$$y = -2x + 6$$
$$y - x = -3$$

Ⓐ $(0, 3)$

Ⓑ $(1, 3)$

Ⓒ $(1, 4)$

Ⓓ $(3, 0)$

3. What is the solution to the system of linear equations?

$$x + 4y = 4$$
$$x - y = -6$$

Ⓐ $(-4, 2)$

Ⓑ $(1, 1)$

Ⓒ $(2, -4)$

Ⓓ $(1, -8)$

4. What is the solution to the system of linear equations?

$$x + y = 4$$
$$4x + y = 0$$

Ⓐ $\left(5\frac{1}{3}, \frac{-4}{3} \right)$

Ⓑ $\left(\frac{-4}{3}, 5\frac{1}{3} \right)$

Ⓒ $\left(\frac{-7}{3}, 6\frac{1}{3} \right)$

Ⓓ $\left(\frac{4}{3}, -5\frac{1}{3} \right)$

5. What is the solution to the system of linear equations shown on this graph?

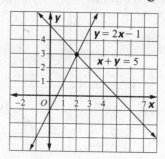

Ⓐ $(-2, 3)$

Ⓑ $(2, 3)$

Ⓒ $(3, 2)$

Ⓓ $(3, 3)$

GPS Practice Pages

6. What is the solution to the system of linear equations shown on this graph?

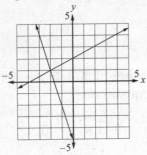

- Ⓐ $(-2, 1)$
- Ⓑ $(-1, -2)$
- Ⓒ $(-2.5, 1)$
- Ⓓ $(1, -2)$

7. What is the solution to the system of linear equations shown on this graph? Determine the equation of the lines to check your answer.

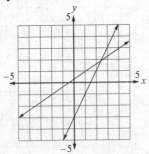

- Ⓐ $\left(2\frac{1}{4}, 1\frac{7}{8}\right)$
- Ⓑ $\left(2\frac{1}{4}, 2\right)$
- Ⓒ $\left(2\frac{1}{2}, 2\right)$
- Ⓓ $\left(2\frac{3}{4}, 2\frac{1}{4}\right)$

8. What are the equations and the solution to the system of linear equations shown on this graph?

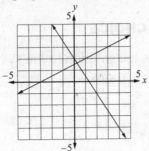

- Ⓐ $y = \frac{1}{2}x + 1\frac{1}{2}$

  $y = -\frac{3}{2}x + 2$

  $\left(\frac{1}{4}, 1\frac{5}{8}\right)$

- Ⓑ $y = \frac{1}{2}x + 1\frac{1}{2}$

  $y = -\frac{3}{2}x + 2$

  $\left(\frac{1}{4}, 1\frac{3}{8}\right)$

- Ⓒ $y = -\frac{1}{2}x + 1\frac{1}{2}$

  $y = \frac{3}{2}x + 2$

  $\left(\frac{1}{4}, 1\frac{5}{8}\right)$

- Ⓓ $y = -\frac{1}{2}x + 1\frac{1}{2}$

  $y = -\frac{3}{2}x + 2$

  $\left(1\frac{5}{8}, \frac{5}{8}\right)$

GPS Practice Pages

M8A5.c
Interpret solutions in problem contexts.

MULTIPLE CHOICE

1. At what point do the graphs of these two functions intersect?
$$y = 3x + 25$$
$$y = 40 - 2x$$

   Ⓐ (3, 34)

   Ⓑ (5, 40)

   Ⓒ (6, 28)

   Ⓓ (34, 3)

2. At what point do the graphs of these two functions intersect?
$$y = 6x + 15$$
$$y + 4x = 0$$

   Ⓐ (−5, −15)

   Ⓑ (−3, 12)

   Ⓒ (−1.5, 6)

   Ⓓ (2.5, −10)

3. Lana is deciding whether to buy a pool pass for the summer. A pass costs $40 and $1 admission for each day. Without a pass, the cost is $5 per day. Use the system of equations to find out the number of days (d) for which the cost (c) is the same with or without a pass.
$$c = \$1d + \$40$$
$$c = \$5d$$

   Ⓐ 5 days

   Ⓑ 10 days

   Ⓒ 20 days

   Ⓓ 40 days

4. Anna's father is 22 years older than Anna. In four years, he will be 3 times as old as Anna is now. Use the system of equations to find both ages now.
$$p = A + 22$$
$$f + 4 = 3A$$

   Ⓐ Anna is 13 and her father is 35

   Ⓑ Anna is 14 and her father is 36

   Ⓒ Anna is 15 and her father is 37

   Ⓓ Anna is 16 and her father is 38

5. A garden plot is twice as long as it is wide. A nearby plot is the same width but 15 feet longer. The perimeter of the second plot is 1.5 times the perimeter of the first plot. Use the system of linear equations to determine the dimensions of the smaller plot.
$$p = 6w$$
$$1.5p = 6w + 30$$

   Ⓐ 8 ft. × 16 ft.

   Ⓑ 9 ft. × 18 ft.

   Ⓒ 10 ft. × 20 ft.

   Ⓓ 12 ft. × 22 ft.

6. At what point do the graphs of these two functions intersect?
$$5y + x = 0$$
$$y + 3x = 14$$

   Ⓐ (−1, −5)

   Ⓑ (−1, 5)

   Ⓒ (5, −1)

   Ⓓ (−5, −1)

7. A bus travels from city A to city B at an average speed of 40 miles per hour. A train leaves 2 hours later and arrives at the same time at an average speed of 60 miles per hour. Which set of linear equations can you use to determine the distance between the cities?

Ⓐ $d = 40h$
$d = 60h - 80$

Ⓑ $d = 40h$
$d = 60h + 80$

Ⓒ $d = 40h - 120$
$d = 60h$

Ⓓ $d = 40h$
$d = 60h - 120$

8. You have enough money to buy 4 CDs and 1 game or 1 CD and 2 games. If you have $126, what do the items cost? Use the system of 2 linear equations for your calculation.

$4c + g = \$126$
$2g + c = \$126$

Ⓐ CD = $22; game = $41

Ⓑ CD = $20; game = $53

Ⓒ CD = $18; game = $54

Ⓓ CD = $14; game = $56

M8D1.a
Demonstrate relationships among sets through use of Venn Diagrams.

MULTIPLE CHOICE

Greg asked 200 people at his gym whether they run, lift weights, or both for exercise. He made the Venn diagram to display the results. Use the Venn diagram to answer questions 1–2.

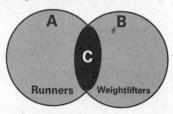

1. What does area *C* represent?

   Ⓐ people who run and lift weights

   Ⓑ people who only run

   Ⓒ people who only lift weights

   Ⓓ people who don't lift weights or run

2. If 120 people said they run, and 100 people said they lift weights, how many people said they both run and lift weights?

   Ⓐ 220   Ⓑ 200

   Ⓒ 100   Ⓓ 20

3. Which description applies to the sets that include the numbers shown in the Venn diagram?

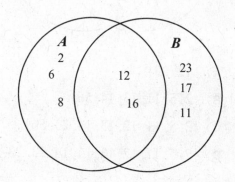

   Ⓐ *A* = numbers less than 10;
      B = odd numbers

   Ⓑ *A* = even numbers;
      B = odd numbers

   Ⓒ *A* = even numbers;
      B = numbers greater than 9

   Ⓓ *A* = numbers less than 10;
      B = numbers greater than 9

GPS Practice Pages

4. What is the union of sets X and Y?

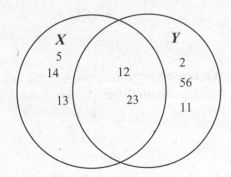

Ⓐ {12, 23}

Ⓑ {2, 5, 11, 13, 14, 56}

Ⓒ {2, 5, 11, 12, 13, 14, 23, 56}

Ⓓ {2, 5, 11, 12, 12, 13, 14, 23, 23, 56}

5. Which sets include the numbers shown in the diagram below?

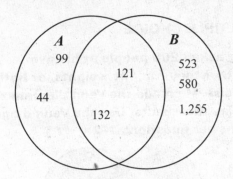

Ⓐ A = repeating digits;
B = greater than 500

Ⓑ A = less than 250;
B = greater than 250

Ⓒ A = divisible by 11;
B = greater than 500

Ⓓ A = divisible by 11;
B = greater than 100

6. What is the intersection of sets *X* and *Y*?

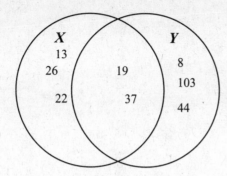

Ⓐ {19, 37}

Ⓑ {8, 13, 22, 26, 44, 103}

Ⓒ {8, 13, 19, 22, 26, 37, 44, 103}

Ⓓ {8, 13, 19, 19, 22, 26, 37, 37, 44, 103}

7. Which of the following numbers belongs in the shaded part of the Venn diagram?

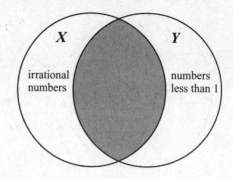

Ⓐ $\sqrt{5}$

Ⓑ $0.\overline{3}$

Ⓒ 0.00059

Ⓓ $\frac{1}{\pi}$

GPS Practice Pages

8. Which sets are displayed in this Venn diagram?

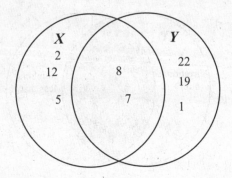

Ⓐ $X = \{2, 5, 12\}$
    $Y = \{1, 7, 8, 19, 22\}$

Ⓑ $X = \{2, 5, 7, 8, 12\}$
    $Y = \{1, 7, 8, 19, 22\}$

Ⓒ $X = \{2, 5, 7, 8, 12\}$
    $Y = \{1, 19, 22\}$

Ⓓ $X = \{2, 5, 7, 8, 12\}$
    $Y = \{1, 2, 5, 7, 8, 12, 19, 22\}$

M8D1.b

Determine subsets, complements, intersection, and union of sets.

MULTIPLE CHOICE

1. Which of the following is not a subset of the set: {0, 1, 2, 3, 4, 5, 6, 7, 8}

   Ⓐ {1, 8}

   Ⓑ {0, 1, 3, 8}

   Ⓒ {0, 1, 2, 3, 4, 5, 6, 7, 8}

   Ⓓ {all positive numbers < 5}

2. For the sets A = {all even integers} and B = {all odd integers}, what is the union of (A and B)?

   Ⓐ {all positive numbers}

   Ⓑ {all numbers}

   Ⓒ {all integers}

   Ⓓ null set

3. The universe for sets C and D is all positive integers less than or equal to 20. For the sets C = {3, 4, 5, 6, 7, 17, 18, 19} and D = {13, 14, 15, 16, 17, 18}, what is the complement of C and D?

   Ⓐ {17, 18}

   Ⓑ {3 ,4, 5, 6, 7, 13, 14, 15, 16, 17, 18, 19}

   Ⓒ {1, 2, 8, 9, 10, 11, 12}

   Ⓓ {1, 2, 8, 9, 10, 11, 12, 20}

4. For the sets A = {33, 36, 37, 40, 46} and B = {35, 36, 40, 49}, which of these statements is not true?

   Ⓐ {36} is the intersection of A and B

   Ⓑ {33, 35, 36, 37, 40, 46, 49} is the union of A and B

   Ⓒ {36, 37, 40} is a subset of A but not a subset of B

   Ⓓ {36, 40} is a subset of A and a subset of B

5. Set X = {all rational numbers} and Y = {all numbers}. Which of the following statements is true?

   Ⓐ Set X is a subset of Set Y

   Ⓑ Set Y is a subset of Set X

   Ⓒ Set X is identical to Set Y

   Ⓓ Set X is the complement of Set Y

6. For the sets A = {all even integers} and B = {all odd integers}, what is the complement of (A and B)?

   Ⓐ {all rational numbers}

   Ⓑ {all non-integer numbers}

   Ⓒ {all integers}

   Ⓓ {all irrational numbers}

GPS Practice Pages

7. For the sets $C = \{1, 4, 8, 9, 15, 17, 18, 19\}$ and $D = \{15, 17, 18, 22\}$, which of the following sets is not a subset of either set?

Ⓐ $\{15, 17, 18\}$

Ⓑ $\{1, 4, 9, 15, 17\}$

Ⓒ $\{1, 9, 15, 17, 22\}$

Ⓓ $\{17, 18, 22\}$

8. For the sets $Y = \{2, 4, 6, 8, 10, 12\}$ and $Z = \{6, 8, 10, 12, 14, 16, 18\}$, which of the following sets is a subset of both sets?

Ⓐ $\{2, 8, 18\}$

Ⓑ $\{4, 6, 12\}$

Ⓒ $\{6, 10, 16\}$

Ⓓ $\{8, 12\}$

M8D1.c

Use set notation to denote elements of a set.

MULTIPLE CHOICE

1. For sets A and B, determine the value $A \cup B$.
$$A = \{1, 2, 3, 4\}$$
$$B = \{4, 5, 6, 7\}$$

   Ⓐ $\{4\}$

   Ⓑ $\{1, 2, 3, 4, 5, 6, 7\}$

   Ⓒ $\{1, 2, 3, 4, 4, 5, 6, 7\}$

   Ⓓ $\{8, 9, 10, 11, ...\}$

2. For sets R and S, determine the value $R \cap S$.
$$R = \{-4, -1, 2, 3, 5\}$$
$$S = \{1, 2, 3, 4, 5, 6\}$$

   Ⓐ $\{1, 2, 3, 4, 5\}$

   Ⓑ $\{2, 3, 5\}$

   Ⓒ $\{-4, -1, 1, 2, 3, 4, 5, 6\}$

   Ⓓ $\{-4, -3, -2, -1, 0, 1, 2, 3, 4, 5, 6\}$

3. For sets A and B, determine the value of $A \cup B$.
$$A = \{8, 12, 14, 16, 17, 21, 24\}$$
$$B = \{5, 6, 8, 14, 18, 21, 22\}$$

   Ⓐ $A \cup B = \{8, 14, 21\}$

   Ⓑ $A \cup B = \{5, 6, 12, 16, 17, 18, 22, 24\}$

   Ⓒ $A \cup B = \{5, 6, 8, 12, 14, 16, 17, 18, 21, 22, 24\}$

   Ⓓ $A \cup B = \{5, 6, 8, 8, 12, 14, 14, 16, 17, 18, 21, 21, 22, 24\}$

4. For sets A and B, determine the value $A \cap B$.
$$A = \{2, 5, 8, 11, 14, 17, 22\}$$
$$B = \{3, 6, 8, 14, 15, 19, 22\}$$

   Ⓐ $A \cap B = \{8, 14, 22\}$

   Ⓑ $A \cap B = \{2, 5, 11, 15, 17, 19\}$

   Ⓒ $A \cap B = \{2, 3, 5, 6, 8, 11, 14, 15, 17, 19, 22\}$

   Ⓓ $A \cap B = \{2, 3, 5, 6, 8, 8, 11, 14, 14, 15, 17, 19, 22, 22\}$

5. For sets W and X, which of the following statements is true?.
$$W = \{3, 6, 7\}$$
$$X = \{1, 3, 6, 7, 15, 16, 18\}$$

   Ⓐ $\sim W = X$

   Ⓑ $X = W$

   Ⓒ $X \subset W$

   Ⓓ $W \subset X$

6. For sets C and D, determine which statement is true.
$$C = \{1, 4, 7, 10, 13\}$$
$$D = \{2, 5, 7, 9, 11\}$$

   Ⓐ $C \cap D = \{1, 2, 4, 7, 9, 10, 11, 13\}$

   Ⓑ $C \cup D = \{1, 2, 4, 7, 9, 10, 11, 13\}$

   Ⓒ $C \subset D$

   Ⓓ $D \in C$

GPS Practice Pages

7. For two sets A and B, which condition below is not true if $A = B$.

Ⓐ $A \cup B = A \cap B$

Ⓑ $A \subset B$

Ⓒ $B \subset A$

Ⓓ $A \cap B = $ null set

8. For sets C and D and E, determine $C \cap D \cap E$.

$C = \{1, 3, 5, 7, 9, 11\}$
$D = \{7, 9, 11, 13, 15\}$
$E = \{11, 13, 15, 17, 19\}$

Ⓐ $\{11\}$

Ⓑ $\{11, 13\}$

Ⓒ $\{7, 9, 11, 13, 15\}$

Ⓓ $\{1, 3, 5, 7, 9, 11, 13, 15, 17, 19\}$

M8D2.a

Use tree diagrams to find the number of outcomes.

MULTIPLE CHOICE

Use this tree diagram to answer questions 1 and 2

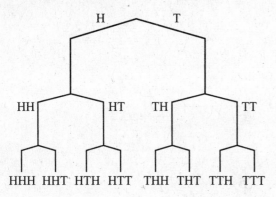

Use this tree diagram to answer questions 3 and 4

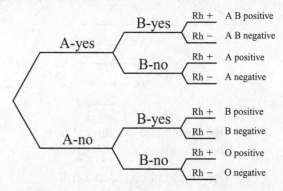

1. The tree diagram above shows the results of three successive coin tosses. Of the eight possible result combinations, how many include exactly two coins showing heads?

   (A) 1

   (B) 2

   (C) 3

   (D) 4

2. What fraction of the possible outcomes includes one or more coins showing tails?

   (A) $\frac{1}{8}$

   (B) $\frac{1}{2}$

   (C) $\frac{3}{4}$

   (D) $\frac{7}{8}$

3. Blood types are used to determine whether a person can safely receive a transfusion from another person. There are three antigens, substances that affect the body's reaction to the blood, labeled A, B and Rh. The tree diagram shows combinations of antigens (presence indicated by yes or +, absence by no or −). If blood from different people can contain any combination from no antigens to all three antigens, how many blood types are possible?

   (A) 3

   (B) 4

   (C) 8

   (D) 16

4. A person can safely receive a transfusion only if the new blood does not contain any antigen that does not exist in the recipient's blood. How many blood types can a person with B-positive blood accept?

   (A) 1   (B) 4

   (C) 6   (D) 8

GPS Practice Pages

5. A bicycle shop sells a certain model of bike in several combinations. Which of the following situations could be represented by this tree diagram?

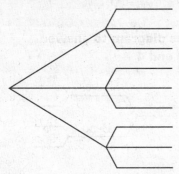

Ⓐ One frame choice, three color choices, three wheel size choices

Ⓑ Two frame choices, two color choices, three wheel size choices

Ⓒ Two frame choices, two color choices, two wheel size choices

Ⓓ Three frame choices, two color choices, one wheel size choice

6. You are buying notebooks for school. The store has a choice of one-subject or three-subject notebooks that are available in red, yellow, blue, or green covers. Which tree diagram below could you use to find out how many choices are possible?

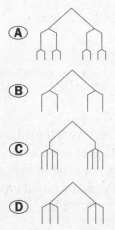

7. A sandwich shop offers two types of bread, 3 choices of meat, and 2 choices of cheese. Which tree diagram could be used to determine the number of possible sandwich choices that have one meat and one cheese?

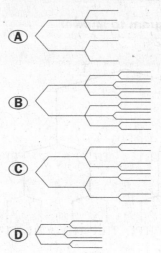

8. Your family is planning a trip to a distant city. You can either fly or take a train to the city. When you get there, you can choose travel from the station by cab, bus, or rental car. Finally, you must choose one of three hotel chains for you stay. How many different combinations of travel and accommodations do you have to choose from?

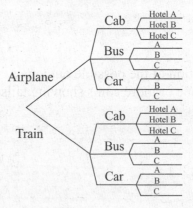

Ⓐ 8

Ⓑ 9

Ⓒ 16

Ⓓ 18

M8D2.b

Apply addition and multiplication counting principles.

MULTIPLE CHOICE

1. What is the total number of possible combinations for abbreviations consisting of two vowels followed by one consonant? (Use 5 vowels and 21 consonants.)

   Ⓐ 31

   Ⓑ 105

   Ⓒ 210

   Ⓓ 525

2. A car model is produced in three body types, with two different engines and six choices of color. How many combinations of body, engine, and color are available?

   Ⓐ 11

   Ⓑ 36

   Ⓒ 72

   Ⓓ 120

3. A filing system assigns an identifier to each file. The identifier consists of one letter followed by two numbers. How many possible file identifiers exist?

   Ⓐ 46

   Ⓑ 100

   Ⓒ 2,600

   Ⓓ 26,000

4. A second filing system also assigns an identifier consisting of one letter followed by two numbers, but the two numbers must be different. How many possible file identifiers exist for this system?

   Ⓐ 45

   Ⓑ 2,340

   Ⓒ 2,600

   Ⓓ 23,400

5. The basic unit of DNA is made of a sequence of four amino acids. There are four possible amino acids for each position in the sequence. How many different units are possible?

   Ⓐ 16

   Ⓑ 32

   Ⓒ 64

   Ⓓ 256

6. How many different 7-digit phone numbers can exist if 0 cannot be the first number?

   Ⓐ 70,000

   Ⓑ 9,000,000

   Ⓒ 10,000,000

   Ⓓ 90,000,000

GPS Practice Pages

7. The cafeteria has 3 choices of salad, 4 choices of entrée, and 3 choices of beverage. How many meal combinations are available?

Ⓐ 10

Ⓑ 30

Ⓒ 36

Ⓓ 144

8. How many combinations can be made for a license plate number that has 2 letters followed by 4 numbers?

Ⓐ 2,600

Ⓑ 26,000

Ⓒ 676,000

Ⓓ 6,760,000

M8D3.a
Find the probability of simple, independent events.

MULTIPLE CHOICE

1. Eight balls numbered from 1 to 8 are placed in an urn. One ball is selected at random. Find the probability that it is *not* number 5.

   Ⓐ $\frac{7}{8}$

   Ⓑ $\frac{3}{4}$

   Ⓒ $\frac{1}{8}$

   Ⓓ $\frac{1}{2}$

2. The table shows the cans of vegetables in Petra's cupboard. If she chooses a can without looking, what is the probability that it is a can of beets?

cans of beets	4
cans of carrots	3
cans of lima beans	4

   Ⓐ $\frac{1}{4}$

   Ⓑ $\frac{4}{11}$

   Ⓒ $\frac{7}{11}$

   Ⓓ none of these

3. Fourteen balls numbered from 1 to 14 are placed in a basket. One ball is selected at random. What is the probability that it is *not* number 3?

   Ⓐ $\frac{6}{7}$

   Ⓑ $\frac{13}{14}$

   Ⓒ $\frac{1}{14}$

   Ⓓ $\frac{3}{14}$

4. The table shows the drink preferences of 50 shoppers at a mall. What is the probability that 1 shopper, selected at random from the 50 surveyed, preferred either Drink A or Drink B?

Drink	Number of Shoppers
A	5
B	6
C	13
D	11
E	15

   Ⓐ $\frac{3}{25}$

   Ⓑ $\frac{3}{250}$

   Ⓒ $\frac{8}{25}$

   Ⓓ $\frac{11}{50}$

GPS Practice Pages

5. If you spin the spinner, what is the probability of the pointer landing on *B*?

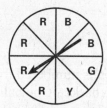

   Ⓐ $\frac{1}{4}$

   Ⓑ 1

   Ⓒ $\frac{1}{2}$

   Ⓓ $\frac{3}{8}$

6. What is the probability of drawing a red ten from a deck of 52 playing cards?

   Ⓐ $\frac{1}{13}$

   Ⓑ $\frac{1}{26}$

   Ⓒ $\frac{1}{50}$

   Ⓓ $\frac{2}{39}$

7. You work at a T-shirt printing business. Of 4,600 T-shirts shipped, 414 are printed improperly. What is the experimental probability that a T-shirt is printed improperly?

   Ⓐ 9%

   Ⓑ 90%

   Ⓒ 10.1%

   Ⓓ 11.1%

8. You work at a CD duplication business. Of 10,000 CDs shipped, 182 have errors. What is the experimental probability that a CD is manufactured correctly?

   Ⓐ 1.82%

   Ⓑ 97.3%

   Ⓒ 98.18%

   Ⓓ 3.72%

M8D3.b

Find the probability of compound, independent events.

MULTIPLE CHOICE

1. What is the probability of rolling a 12 in a single roll of two dice?

    (A) $\frac{1}{6}$

    (B) $\frac{1}{11}$

    (C) $\frac{1}{12}$

    (D) $\frac{1}{36}$

2. At a school bazaar, the principal is going to randomly draw one name to win a prize from the names of the 100 students who entered the drawing. After the drawing, the name is replaced. If there are 3 drawings, what is the probability of one person winning all 3 prizes?

    (A) $\frac{1}{300}$

    (B) $\frac{1}{10,000}$

    (C) $\frac{1}{1,000,000}$

    (D) $\frac{3}{1,000,000}$

3. What is the probability of tossing a coin and getting heads 5 times in a row?

    (A) $\frac{1}{5}$

    (B) $\frac{1}{32}$

    (C) $\frac{1}{64}$

    (D) $\frac{1}{100,000}$

4. If you have tossed a coin 3 times, getting heads each time, what is the probability that the next two tosses will both be heads also?

    (A) $\frac{1}{4}$

    (B) $\frac{1}{16}$

    (C) $\frac{1}{32}$

    (D) 0

5. A and B are independent events. If $P(A) = 0.3$ and $P(B) = 0.2$, what is the value of $P(A \text{ and } B)$?

    (A) 0.06

    (B) 0.2

    (C) 0.5

    (D) 0.6

6. A and B are independent events. If $P(A) = 0.08$ and $P(A \text{ and } B) = 0.0048$, what is the value of $P(B)$?

    (A) 0.000384

    (B) 0.06

    (C) 0.4

    (D) 0.6

7. You ask two people to choose a circle from the group of circles below. Assuming that the choices are random, what is the probability that both people will choose a gray circle?

    Ⓐ 0.016

    Ⓑ 0.08

    Ⓒ 0.16

    Ⓓ 0.4

8. A bag contains 20 lettered tiles. The number of tiles with several letters are shown on the table below. If you replace the letter after each draw, what is the probability of drawing C-A-T in that order?

Letter	Number of tiles
A	10
C	5
T	5

    Ⓐ $\dfrac{1}{10}$

    Ⓑ $\dfrac{1}{20}$

    Ⓒ $\dfrac{1}{32}$

    Ⓓ $\dfrac{1}{125}$

GPS Practice Pages

M8D4.a

Gather data that can be modeled with a linear function.

MULTIPLE CHOICE

1. The table shows the amount of time several students spent watching TV and their test grades. Which scatter plot describes the data and the relationship, if any?

Weekly TV (h)	6	12	18	24	30	36
Grade (%)	95	90	75	80	65	60

Ⓐ
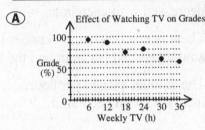
More hours spent watching TV may increase grades.

Ⓑ
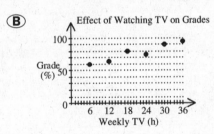
More hours spent watching TV may reduce grades.

Ⓒ
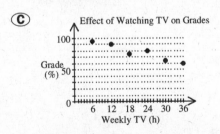
More hours spent watching TV may reduce grades.

Ⓓ none of these

2. The scatter plot shows the relationship between the number of years a company was in business and the number of employees. Which is the best conclusion based on the plot?

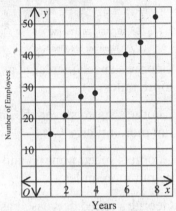

Ⓐ The number of employees stayed the same from year to year.

Ⓑ The number of employees increased each year.

Ⓒ The number of employees decreased each year.

Ⓓ The number of employees increased some years and decreased other years.

GPS Practice Pages

3. The scatter plot shows the relationship between the number of total miles run, and the average speed that George ran in miles per hour during a long distance race. Which is the best conclusion based on the plot?

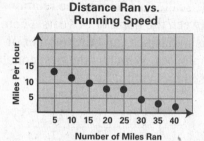

**Distance Ran vs.
Running Speed**

Miles Per Hour

Number of Miles Ran

Ⓐ George's speed increased as he ran more miles.

Ⓑ George's speed stayed the same as he ran more miles.

Ⓒ George's speed went up and down as he ran more miles.

Ⓓ George's speed decreased as he ran more miles.

4. The scatter plot shows the relationship between the number of hours worked, and the amount of money earned per hour at a hardware store. Which is the best conclusion based on the plot?

**Hours Worked
vs.
Earnings Per Hour**

Money Earned
That Hour

Hours Worked

Ⓐ The amount earned per hour stayed constant from hour to hour.

Ⓑ The amount earned per hour decreased with each hour.

Ⓒ There is no correlation between the amount earned per hour and the hour.

Ⓓ The amount earned per hour increased with each hour.

5. On a long trip, Leonard recorded the number of miles driven in his family's car and the amount of gas used. The table below shows the distance traveled compared to the total amount of gas used. Can Leonard's data be modeled by a linear function and, if yes, what is the function?

Miles	150	400	700	1000	1200
Gallons	6	16	28	40	48

Ⓐ no

Ⓑ yes; miles × 25 = gallons

Ⓒ yes; miles = gallons × 25

Ⓓ yes; miles = gallons × 40

6. Max wants buy discount tickets for a local theater. There is a handling charge and a charge per ticket. The table below shows the cost of several ticket book options. Can the costs be modeled by a linear function and, if yes, what is the function?

Number of tickets	5	10	15	20	25
Total Cost	$30	$55	$80	$105	$130

Ⓐ no

Ⓑ yes; Cost = number of tickets × $5

Ⓒ yes; Cost = number of tickets × $5 − $5

Ⓓ yes; Cost = number of tickets × $5 + $5

7. Maria checks the price of jars of peanut butter at the grocery store and makes a table of the size of the jar and the cost. Can the costs be modeled by a linear function and, if yes, what is the function?

Weight of jar (oz.)	8	16	24	32	40
Cost	$1.25	$2.75	$3.75	$4.25	$5.00

Ⓐ no

Ⓑ yes; Cost = weight (oz) × $0.12

Ⓒ yes; Cost = weight (oz) × $0.10 + $0.45

Ⓓ yes; Cost = weight (oz) × $0.125 + $0.25

8. A scatter plot of the distance between a train and a station shows a strong negative relationship. What can you conclude about the motion of the train?

Ⓐ The train is traveling away from the station at a constant speed.

Ⓑ The train is traveling toward the station at a constant speed.

Ⓒ The train is stationary at a point away from the station.

Ⓓ The train is stationary at the station.

M8D4.b

Estimate and determine a line of best fit from a scatter plot.

MULTIPLE CHOICE

1. Which of these equations best describes the line of best fit for the data on the scatter plot?

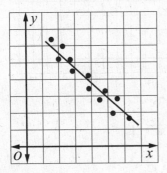

  Ⓐ $y = -x - 8$

  Ⓑ $y = -x + 8$

  Ⓒ $y = x - 8$

  Ⓓ $y = x + 8$

2. Which equation represents the line of best fit for this scatter plot?

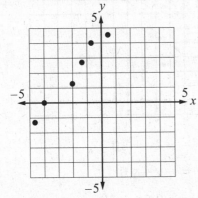

  Ⓐ $y = x + 4$

  Ⓑ $y = x - 4$

  Ⓒ $y = 2x + 2$

  Ⓓ $y = 4x - 4$

3. Which equation represents the line of best fit for this scatter plot?

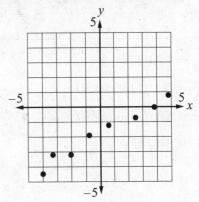

  Ⓐ $y = -\frac{1}{2}x - 2$

  Ⓑ $y = \frac{1}{2}x - 2$

  Ⓒ $y = 2x - \frac{1}{2}$

  Ⓓ $y = 2x + \frac{1}{2}$

4. Which of these equations describes the line that best fits the data on the scatter plot?

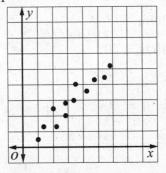

  Ⓐ $y = -x$

  Ⓑ $y = x - 1$

  Ⓒ $y = x$

  Ⓓ $y = x + 2$

GPS Practice Pages

5. Which equation describes the line of best fit of this scatter plot? Use c = cost in dollars and l = length.

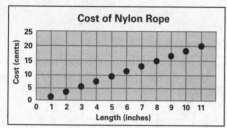

A $c = \$0.02l$

B $c = \$0.02l + \$0.50$

C $c = \$0.02l - \$0.50$

D $c = \$0.20l$

6. Which equation describes the line of best fit of this scatter plot? Use S = sales and y = years.

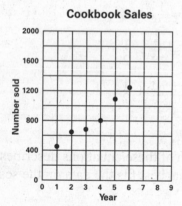

A $S = 200y$

B $S = 200y + 50$

C $S = 200y - 200$

D $S = 200y + 200$

7. Estimate the line of best fit for this scatter plot.

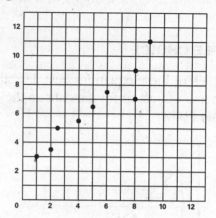

A $y = 3x$

B $y = x + 1$

C $y = x + 3$

D $y = 2x + 3$

8. Estimate the line of best fit for this scatter plot.

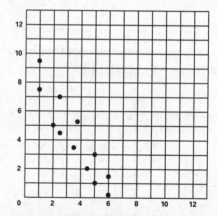

A $y = -2x + 10$

B $y = -x + 10$

C $y = -0.5x + 10$

D $y = x + 10$

Grade 8 Georgia CRCT Practice Test
Answer Sheet

1. Ⓐ Ⓑ Ⓒ Ⓓ   36. Ⓐ Ⓑ Ⓒ Ⓓ
2. Ⓐ Ⓑ Ⓒ Ⓓ   37. Ⓐ Ⓑ Ⓒ Ⓓ
3. Ⓐ Ⓑ Ⓒ Ⓓ   38. Ⓐ Ⓑ Ⓒ Ⓓ
4. Ⓐ Ⓑ Ⓒ Ⓓ   39. Ⓐ Ⓑ Ⓒ Ⓓ
5. Ⓐ Ⓑ Ⓒ Ⓓ   40. Ⓐ Ⓑ Ⓒ Ⓓ
6. Ⓐ Ⓑ Ⓒ Ⓓ   41. Ⓐ Ⓑ Ⓒ Ⓓ
7. Ⓐ Ⓑ Ⓒ Ⓓ   42. Ⓐ Ⓑ Ⓒ Ⓓ
8. Ⓐ Ⓑ Ⓒ Ⓓ   43. Ⓐ Ⓑ Ⓒ Ⓓ
9. Ⓐ Ⓑ Ⓒ Ⓓ   44. Ⓐ Ⓑ Ⓒ Ⓓ
10. Ⓐ Ⓑ Ⓒ Ⓓ   45. Ⓐ Ⓑ Ⓒ Ⓓ
11. Ⓐ Ⓑ Ⓒ Ⓓ   46. Ⓐ Ⓑ Ⓒ Ⓓ
12. Ⓐ Ⓑ Ⓒ Ⓓ   47. Ⓐ Ⓑ Ⓒ Ⓓ
13. Ⓐ Ⓑ Ⓒ Ⓓ   48. Ⓐ Ⓑ Ⓒ Ⓓ
14. Ⓐ Ⓑ Ⓒ Ⓓ   49. Ⓐ Ⓑ Ⓒ Ⓓ
15. Ⓐ Ⓑ Ⓒ Ⓓ   50. Ⓐ Ⓑ Ⓒ Ⓓ
16. Ⓐ Ⓑ Ⓒ Ⓓ   51. Ⓐ Ⓑ Ⓒ Ⓓ
17. Ⓐ Ⓑ Ⓒ Ⓓ   52. Ⓐ Ⓑ Ⓒ Ⓓ
18. Ⓐ Ⓑ Ⓒ Ⓓ   53. Ⓐ Ⓑ Ⓒ Ⓓ
19. Ⓐ Ⓑ Ⓒ Ⓓ   54. Ⓐ Ⓑ Ⓒ Ⓓ
20. Ⓐ Ⓑ Ⓒ Ⓓ   55. Ⓐ Ⓑ Ⓒ Ⓓ
21. Ⓐ Ⓑ Ⓒ Ⓓ   56. Ⓐ Ⓑ Ⓒ Ⓓ
22. Ⓐ Ⓑ Ⓒ Ⓓ   57. Ⓐ Ⓑ Ⓒ Ⓓ
23. Ⓐ Ⓑ Ⓒ Ⓓ   58. Ⓐ Ⓑ Ⓒ Ⓓ
24. Ⓐ Ⓑ Ⓒ Ⓓ   59. Ⓐ Ⓑ Ⓒ Ⓓ
25. Ⓐ Ⓑ Ⓒ Ⓓ   60. Ⓐ Ⓑ Ⓒ Ⓓ
26. Ⓐ Ⓑ Ⓒ Ⓓ   61. Ⓐ Ⓑ Ⓒ Ⓓ
27. Ⓐ Ⓑ Ⓒ Ⓓ   62. Ⓐ Ⓑ Ⓒ Ⓓ
28. Ⓐ Ⓑ Ⓒ Ⓓ   63. Ⓐ Ⓑ Ⓒ Ⓓ
29. Ⓐ Ⓑ Ⓒ Ⓓ   64. Ⓐ Ⓑ Ⓒ Ⓓ
30. Ⓐ Ⓑ Ⓒ Ⓓ   65. Ⓐ Ⓑ Ⓒ Ⓓ
31. Ⓐ Ⓑ Ⓒ Ⓓ   66. Ⓐ Ⓑ Ⓒ Ⓓ
32. Ⓐ Ⓑ Ⓒ Ⓓ   67. Ⓐ Ⓑ Ⓒ Ⓓ
33. Ⓐ Ⓑ Ⓒ Ⓓ   68. Ⓐ Ⓑ Ⓒ Ⓓ
34. Ⓐ Ⓑ Ⓒ Ⓓ   69. Ⓐ Ⓑ Ⓒ Ⓓ
35. Ⓐ Ⓑ Ⓒ Ⓓ   70. Ⓐ Ⓑ Ⓒ Ⓓ

CRCT Practice Test

Grade 8 Georgia CRCT Practice Test

1. Which of these numbers is the same as $\sqrt{0.49}$?

   A 0.07

   B -0.7

   C 0.23

   D 0.007

2. What is the value of x if the area of the square is 144 m^2?

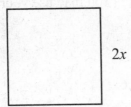

2x

   A 4 m

   B 6 m

   C 8 m

   D 12 m

3. Match the point on the line with the correct number below.

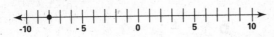

   A $\sqrt{-64}$

   B $-\sqrt{8}$

   C $\sqrt{8}$

   D $\sqrt{64}$

4. Which statement below best describes the number statement?

$$-\sqrt{\frac{1}{144}} = \frac{1}{12}$$

   A always true

   B never true

   C sometimes true

   D cannot be determined

5. The area of a square vacant lot is 2500 m^2. Which of the following statements can be used to calculate the length of one side?

   A $\sqrt{2500 \text{ m}^2} = 50$ m

   B $\sqrt{2500 \text{ m}^2} = -50$ m

   C $\sqrt{2500 \text{ m}^2} = 50$ m or -50 m

   D $\sqrt{2500 \text{ m}^2} = 500$ m

6. A carpet installer says that you will need 228 square feet of carpet for your room. Knowing that the room is square, estimate the length of one side of the room.

   A 12 feet

   B 15 feet

   C 18 feet

   D 21 feet

7. Without using a calculator, approximate the square root to the nearest hundredth.
$$\sqrt{0.0909}$$

   A 0.03

   B 0.09

   C 0.30

   D 0.99

CRCT Practice Test

8. Evaluate. $\sqrt{81} + \sqrt{144}$

  A 12   **B** 15

  C 21   **D** $\sqrt{225}$

9. Which of these numbers is an irrational number?

  A $3.36\overline{7}$

  B $\sqrt{33}$

  C $\sqrt{\dfrac{9}{64}}$

  D $\dfrac{11}{31}$

10. Simplify the expression.
$$y^2 + 7y^2 + 4y^3 + 6y^3$$

  A $10y^3 + 7y^2$

  B $8y^3 + 10y^2$

  C $10y^3 + 8y^2$

  D $18y^5$

11. Radio signals travel at a rate of 3.00 $\times 10^8$ meters per second. How many seconds will it take for a radio signal to travel from a satellite to the surface of Earth if the satellite is orbiting at a height of 2.16×10^8 meters?

  A 0.72 seconds   **B** 7.20 seconds

  C 64.8 seconds   **D** 6.48 seconds

12. What is 4.25×10^3 written in standard form?

  A 425   **B** 4,250

  C 42,500   **D** 425,000

13. The formula $v = \sqrt{64h}$ can be used to find the velocity, v, in feet per second of an object that has fallen h feet. Find the velocity of an object that has fallen 120 feet. Round your answer to the nearest hundredth.

  A 701.06 feet per second

  B 7,680 feet per second

  C 960 feet per second

  D 87.64 feet per second

14. To the nearest tenth, what is the value of $\sqrt{2633}$? (You may use your calculator.)

  A 16.2

  B 51.3

  C 88.6

  D 162.2

15. Which equation below represents a line that is perpendicular to the line represented by $y = 3x + 2$?

  A $y \;\; 3x - 2$

  B $y = -3x + 2$

  C $y = \dfrac{1}{3}x + 2$

  D $y = -\dfrac{1}{3}x + 2$

16. What is the measure of $\angle 2$?

  A 180°

  B 140°

  C 90°

  D 40°

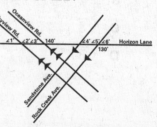

CRCT Practice Test

17. If the two horizontal lines are parallel, what is $m\angle A$?

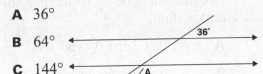

   A 36°

   B 64°

   C 144°

   D 166°

18. What is the value of x?

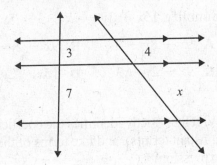

   A 8

   B $9\dfrac{1}{3}$

   C $10\dfrac{2}{3}$

   D 12

19. $\triangle ABC$ is congruent with $\triangle XYZ$. Which of the congruence statements below is true?

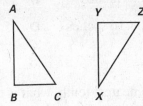

   A $\overline{AB} \cong \overline{XY}; \angle C \cong \angle Z$

   B $\overline{BA} \cong \overline{XZ}; \angle C \cong \angle Z$

   C $\overline{AB} \cong \overline{YZ}; \angle A \cong \angle X$

   D $\overline{CA} \cong \overline{ZX}; \angle A \cong \angle Y$

20. The two polygons below are congruent. Which of the following correctly shows corresponding sides and identifies the measures of the unknown angles?

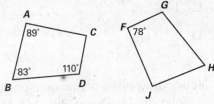

   A $\overline{AB} \cong \overline{GH}; \overline{BD} \cong \overline{FJ};$
      $m\angle J = 83°; m\angle H = 89°$

   B $\overline{AB} \cong \overline{FJ}; \overline{CA} \cong \overline{HG};$
      $m\angle J = 83°; m\angle H = 78°$

   C $\overline{AC} \cong \overline{JF}; \overline{AB} \cong \overline{JH};$
      $m\angle J = 89°; m\angle G = 110°$

   D $\overline{AB} \cong \overline{JF}; \overline{BD} \cong \overline{GH};$
      $m\angle J = 83°; m\angle H = 89°$

21. Standing next to each other, a woman who is 64 inches tall casts a 83.2 inch shadow and her son casts a 50.7 inch shadow. What is the height of the son to the nearest inch?

A 50.7 inches   **B** 39 inches

C 108.16 inches   **D** 65.91 inches

22. To the nearest tenth, what is the diagonal of this rectangle?

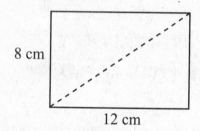

8 cm

12 cm

A 9.8 cm

B 13.0 cm

C 14.4 cm

D 18.0 cm

23. Henry draws two points on a coordinate plane at $A(-4, 6)$ and $B(2, 14)$. He uses the Pythagorean Theorem to find the distance between the two points. What is the distance between A and B?

A 100 units   **B** 8 units

C 6 units   **D** 10 units

24. Tony plots two points $(1, 10)$ and $(4, 6)$ on a coordinate plane. He measures the distance between the two points. Which shows the distance between the points?

A 25   **B** 6

C $\frac{3}{5}$ **D** 5

25. Joaquim owned so many posters that he couldn't find room for them all, so he picked out 36 of them to sell. After he sold the posters, he still had 30 left. Write an equation to find how many posters Joaquim had to begin with. Then solve the equation.

A $p = 30 \times 36$; 1,080 posters

B $p - 36 = 30$; 66 posters

C $p = 30 - 36$; 6 posters

D none of these

26. Simplify. $15x + 3y - 6x + 3 + 5y$

A $9x + 8y + 3$ **B** $9x - 2y + 3$

C $9x - 2y - 3$ **D** $15x - 2y - 3$

27. Which correctly identifies the coefficients, constant term(s), and like terms of the expression?
$$3x + 2 - 5x - 7$$

A coefficients: 3, 5
constant terms: 2, 7
like terms: $3x$ and $5x$, 2 and 7

B coefficients: 3, 5
constant terms: 2, 7
like terms: $3x$ and 2, 7 and $5x$

C coefficients: 3, -5
constant terms: 2, -7
like terms: $3x$ and $-5x$, 2 and -7

D coefficients: 3, -5
constant terms: 2, -7
like terms: $3x$ and 2, -7 and $-5x$

28. What is the value of x?
$$3x + 35 = 104$$

A 23   **B** 207

C 69   **D** 3

Grade 8 Georgia CRCT Practice Test

29. Irene earns $11.34 per hour. For each full 40-hour week she works, she earns a bonus of $58 as well. If w stands for the number of full weeks that she works and t stands for the total she has earned, which equation can be used to find out how much she earns in w weeks?

A $t = 40w \times 11.34 + 58$

B $t = w(40 \times 11.34 + 58)$

C $40t = w \times 11.34 + 58$

D none of these

30. Helen owns 6 times as many DVDs as Kate. Kate owns 19 DVDs. How many DVDs does Helen own?

A 25 **B** 144

C 114 **D** none of these

31. Which shows a verbal sentence that describes the inequality, along with the solution?
A number multiplied by 4 is less than 20.

A $4x > 20$; $x > 80$

B $4x > 20$; $x > 5$

C $4x > 20$; $x < 80$

D $4x < 20$; $x < 5$

32. Solve this inequality for x.
$$3 - 2x > 14$$

A $x < 5.5$ **B** $x > 5.5$

C $x < 8.5$ **D** $x \leq 5.5$

33. Which inequality is shown on the number line?

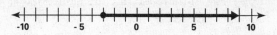

A $x > 3$ **B** $x > -3$

C $x \geq -3$ **D** $x \leq -3$

34. Which problem could be solved using the inequality $2a < 56$?

A Two students split a restaurant bill that came to less than $56.

B The product of a number and 2 is equal to 56.

C Marty earned $56 for 2 hours of work.

D Two shirts came to at least $56.

35. The cost of a school banquet is $95 plus $13 for each person attending. This can be modeled by the equation $C = 13x + 95$ where C represents the total cost in dollars and x is the number of people attending. What is the cost for 75 people?

A $950 **B** $1,070

C $1,145 **D** $1,350

CRCT Practice Test

36. What is the effect on y of an increase in the value of x?

x	−1	1	3	5	7
y	45	41	37	33	29

A an increase in y the same size as the increase in x

B a decrease in y the same size as the increase in x

C a decrease in y twice the size of the increase in x

D a decrease in y of four times the size of the increase in x

37. Which shows an input-output table for the function $y = 6 + 4x$ using the domain −2, −1, 0, 1, and 2?

A
Input x	−2	−1	0	1	2
Output y	4	5	6	7	8

B
Input x	−2	−1	0	1	2
Output y	−2	−1	0	1	2

C
Input x	−2	−1	0	1	2
Output y	−2	2	6	10	14

D
Input x	−2	−1	0	1	2
Output y	2	−2	−6	−10	−14

38. Penelope graphed a function on a coordinate plane. Which graph represents a function of x?

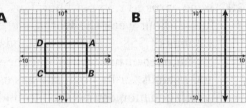
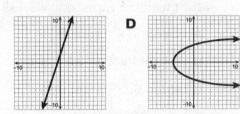

39. Ramon used an equation to calculate the x and y values in the table below. Which equation could he have used?

Input x	2	1	0	1
Output y	15	12	9	6

A $9x + 3y = 9$ **B** $x + 3y = 9$

C $3x + y = 9$ **D** $y = 3x + 9$

40. The table below shows the price for garden soil, depending upon how much is purchased. Which equation is represented by the table?

Soil (cu. yd.)	0	1	2	3	4	5
Cost	20	29	38	47	56	65

A $9y = x + 20$

B $y = 9(x + 20)$

C $y = 9x + 20$

D $y = x + 9(20)$

Grade 8 Georgia CRCT Practice Test

41. Jessica is paid x dollars per hour at her job at the summer camp. She also is paid a bonus of $80 for each 40-hour week she works. The table shows her earnings after several 40-hour weeks. How much will she have earned by the end of week 5?

Week	1	2	3	4	5
Total Earnings	$593.20	$1,186.40	$1,779.60	$2,372.80	

A $513.20

B $2,566.00

C $2,452.80

D $2,966.00

42. The table shows the total balance of Byron's savings account, where x represents the number of weeks and y represents the balance. If the pattern continues each week, which expression would you use to find out his total balance for week 8?

Input x	1	2	3	4	5
Output y	27	42	57	72	87

A $y = x + 15$

B $y = 15x$

C $y = 12x + 15$

D $y = 15x + 12$

43. A single square has 4 sides. If two squares are placed next to each other in a row, the total number of sides is 7. If three squares are placed next to each other in a row, there are 10 sides total. The function table shows the number of sides for up to 5 squares placed next to each other in a row.

Number of Squares x	1	2	3	4	5
Number of Sides y	4	7	10	13	16

Which function rule matches this table?

A $y = 3x$

B $y = 3x + 1$

C $y = 2x + 2$

D $y = 4x - 3$

44. Which describes the pattern of the total number of pencils sold for every packages of 8 sold?

$$8, 16, 24, 28, \dots$$

A Add eight to find the next term.

B Multiply term by eight to find next term.

C Add nine and subtract two to find next term.

D Multiply term by seven to find next term.

45. Jerri graphed the equation of a line onto a coordinate plane and finds that the line passes through the two points below. What is the slope of the line that passes through the points?

$$(-9, -3), (-4, -2)$$

A $\dfrac{1}{5}$ **B** $\dfrac{1}{3}$

C 5 **D** 3

46. Which of these is not a linear function?

A $y = \dfrac{x}{43} - \dfrac{5}{8}$

B $\dfrac{y}{2} = -x + \dfrac{y}{8}$

C $-y = 3$

D $14y = \dfrac{8}{x} + \dfrac{7}{8}$

47. Which table of values represents the function rule $y = -6x + 13$?

A

Input x	1	2	3	4	5
Output y	19	25	31	37	43

B

Input x	1	2	3	4	5
Output y	14	15	16	17	18

C

Input x	1	2	3	4	5
Output y	−6	−12	−18	−24	−30

D

Input x	1	2	3	4	5
Output y	7	1	5	11	17

48. Which function rule relates x and y?

Input x	1	2	3	4	5
Output y	15	14	13	12	11

A $y = -x + 16$ **B** $y = 16x - 1$

C $y = x + 16$ **D** $y = -x - 16$

49. What is the slope of the line on the graph below?

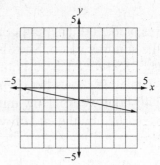

A $-\dfrac{1}{5}$ **B** $-\dfrac{1}{10}$

C $\dfrac{1}{5}$ **D** 5

50. Which shows the intercepts of the graph of the equation?

$$y = 2x - 6$$

A x-intercept: $-\dfrac{1}{3}$, y-intercept: -6

B x-intercept: -3, y-intercept: -6

C x-intercept: $\dfrac{1}{3}$, y-intercept: -6

D x-intercept: 3, y-intercept: -6

51. The cost to mail a first class letter is 39 cents for the first ounce and 24 cents for each additional ounce. The postage for a letter that weighs x ounces can be calculated using the formula:

$$y = \$0.24(x - 1) + \$0.39$$

What do the slope and the y-intercept of this line represent?

A slope – cost for the first ounce; y-intercept – cost of additional ounces

B slope – weight of letter; y-intercept – cost for each ounce after the first

C y-intercept – cost for the first ounce; slope – cost of additional ounces

D y-intercept – number of ounces; slope – cost for each ounce after the first

CRCT Practice Test

52. Which graph represents the equation?

$$y = -\frac{1}{3}x - 1$$

A 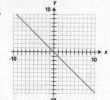   **B**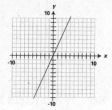

C 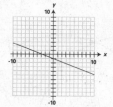   **D**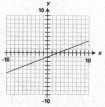

53. Which equation describes this graph?

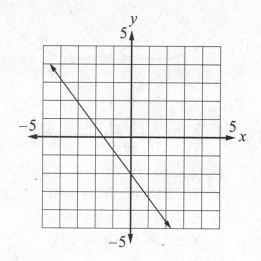

A $3x - 4y = 6$

B $3x + 4y = -6$

C $4x + 3y = 6$

D $4x + 3y = -6$

54. What is the equation of this line?

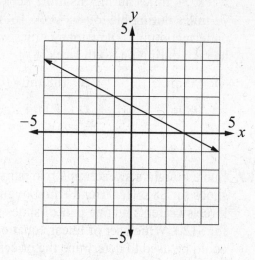

A $y = \frac{1}{2}x + 1\frac{1}{2}$

B $y = -\frac{1}{2}x + 1\frac{1}{2}$

C $y = -2x + 1\frac{1}{2}$

D $y = 2x - 1\frac{1}{2}$

55. Which function is represented by the graph?

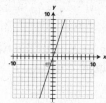

A $y = \frac{x}{4}$ **B** $y = 4x$

C $y = \frac{4}{x}$ **D** $y = x + 4$

CRCT Practice Test

56. Tony bicycles a total of 18 miles during his first week of training for the Five Borough Bike Ride through New York City. He bikes 36 miles during his second week, 54 miles during his third week, and 72 miles during his fourth week. If the pattern continues, how many miles will he bike during his sixth week?

A 90 mi. **B** 108 mi.

C 98 mi. **D** 120 mi.

57. Lucia bought a sweater and two pairs of shoes for $85. Her friend Kim bought three sweaters and one pair of shoes for $120. Which set of linear equations could be used to determine the prices of a sweater (*a*) and of a pair of shoes (*b*)?

A $a + 2b = \$120$
$3a + b = \$85$

B $2b - a = \$85$
$3a - b = \$120$

C $a + 2b = \$85$
$3a + b = \$120$

D $a = 2b - \$85$
$3a + b = \$120$

58. At what point do the graphs to the two lines described by these equations intersect?

$$y = 3x - 14$$
$$y = -2x + 6$$

A $(-2, 4)$

B $(4, -2)$

C $(5, -4)$

D $(6, 4)$

59. Walt is 4 years older than twice his brother's age right now. In 4 years, Walt will be twice as old as his brother. Use a system of linear equations to determine Walt's age now.

A 11 **B** 12

C 14 **D** 16

60. Which sets are displayed in this Venn diagram?

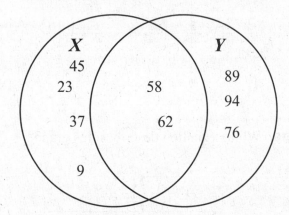

A X = {9, 23, 37, 45}
Y = {76, 89, 94}

B X = {9, 23, 37, 45, 58, 62}
Y = {76, 89, 94}

C X = {9, 23, 37, 45}
Y = {58, 62, 76, 89, 94}

D X = {9, 23, 37, 45, 58, 62}
Y = {58, 62, 76, 89, 94}

61. Rhoda is putting together sets of trading cards. She has 75 baseball cards, 45 football cards, and 60 hockey cards. She wants each set to have an equal number of each type of card. What is the largest number of sets she can make?

A 25 sets **B** 15 sets

C 5 sets **D** 3 sets

62. For sets A and B, determine the value of $A \cap B$.

$A = \{6, 19, 22, 29, 43, 56, 98\}$
$B = \{8, 22, 42, 43, 56, 89, 107\}$

A $A \cap B = \{22, 43, 56\}$

B $A \cap B = \{6, 19, 29, 42, 89, 98, 107\}$

C $A \cap B = \{6, 19, 22, 29, 42, 43, 56, 89, 98, 107\}$

D $A \cap B = \{6, 19, 22, 22, 29, 42, 43, 43, 56, 56, 89, 98, 107\}$

63. Your club is planning an ice cream sundae sale as a fundraiser. The tree diagram below represents the different choices of sundaes. Which of the following combinations could be represented by the diagram?

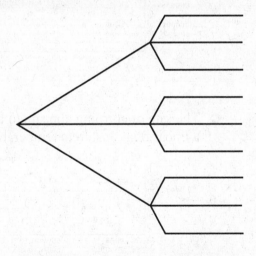

A one size, two flavors, three toppings

B one size, three flavors, three toppings

C two sizes, two flavors, three toppings

D two sizes, three flavors, three toppings

64. The shipping department at a manufacturing company sorts orders using a coded system. The codes for different regions use two letters – one of 5 vowels followed by one of 21 consonants. How many different regions can be coded using this system?

A 21   **B** 26

C 105   **D** 525

65. There are 16 beads in a bag, of which 6 beads are white, 7 beads are yellow, 2 beads are green, and the rest are blue. Jason will choose one bead from the bag without looking. What is the theoretical probability of choosing a blue bead?

A $\dfrac{1}{8}$ **B** $\dfrac{1}{16}$

C $\dfrac{7}{16}$ **D** $\dfrac{1}{2}$

66. Each letter in DECAFFEINATED is written on a separate piece of paper and put into a bag. You randomly choose a piece of paper from the bag. What is the probability of choosing an E?

A $\dfrac{3}{8}$ **B** $\dfrac{1}{8}$

C $\dfrac{3}{13}$ **D** $\dfrac{1}{13}$

CRCT Practice Test

67. You are using this spinner to play a board game. What is the probability that you will spin "Move ahead 1 space" on your first turn followed by "Lose a turn" on your second turn?

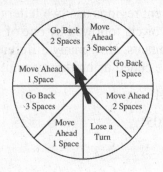

A $\frac{1}{64}$

B $\frac{1}{32}$

C $\frac{1}{8}$

D $\frac{3}{8}$

68. As part of a science project, Lee counted the number of times a cricket chirped in a minute at different times during the day and then measured the temperature in °F. Which scatter plot describes his data and the relationship between the variables?

Temp (°F)	55	57	60	65	68	70
Chirps per minute	62	70	81	100	108	120

A The rate of chirping appears to be unrelated to temperature.

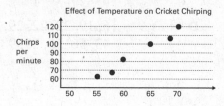

B The rate of chirping appears to be unrelated to temperature.

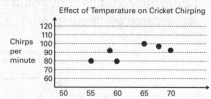

C The rate of chirping appears to have a linear relationship to temperature.

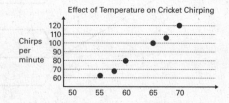

D none of these

Grade 8 Georgia CRCT Practice Test

69. This scatter plot shows the relationship between the number of years (y) a company was in business and the number of employees (e). What equation represents the line of best fit for the graph?

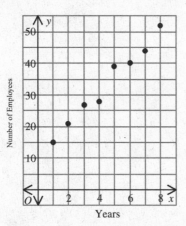

Years

A $e = y + 2$

B $e = 5y$

C $e = 5y + 10$

D $e = 5y + 15$

70. This scatter plot shows the relationship between a student's test score (s) and the number of hours (h) that were spent studying for the test. Which equation shows the line of best fit for this graph?

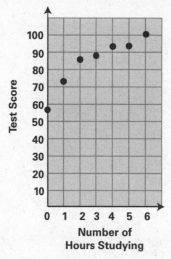

Number of Hours Studying

A $s = 7h + 60$

B $s = 7h - 65$

C $s = \dfrac{h}{7} + 60$

D $s = -\dfrac{h}{7} + 60$

Grade 8 Georgia Diagnostic Scoring Sheet

Georgia Performance Standards	Diagnostic Test	CRCT Practice Test	Test Preparation Workbook
M8N1.a Find square roots of perfect squares.	ITEM 1, 2 CORRECT ___/2	ITEM 1 CORRECT ___/1	1–2
M8N1.b Recognize the (positive) square root of a number as a length of a side of a square with a given area.	ITEM 3, 4 CORRECT ___/2	ITEM 2 CORRECT ___/1	3–4
M8N1.c Recognize square roots as points and as lengths on a number line.	ITEM 5, 6 CORRECT ___/2	ITEM 3 CORRECT ___/1	5–6
M8N1.d Understand that the square root of 0 is 0 and that every positive number has two square roots that are opposite in sign.	ITEM 7, 8 CORRECT ___/2	ITEM 4 CORRECT ___/1	7–8
M8N1.e Recognize and use the radical symbol to denote the positive square root of a positive number.	ITEM 9, 10 CORRECT ___/2	ITEM 5 CORRECT ___/1	9–10
M8N1.f Estimate square roots of positive numbers.	ITEM 11, 12 CORRECT ___/2	ITEM 6, 7 CORRECT ___/2	11–12
M8N1.g Simplify, add, subtract, multiply, and divide expressions containing square roots.	ITEM 13, 14 CORRECT ___/2	ITEM 8 CORRECT ___/1	13–14
M8N1.h Distinguish between rational and irrational numbers.	ITEM 15, 16 CORRECT ___/2	ITEM 9 CORRECT ___/1	15–16
M8N1.i Simplify expressions containing integer exponents.	ITEM 17, 18 CORRECT ___/2	ITEM 10 CORRECT ___/1	17–18

Grade 8 Georgia Diagnostic Scoring Sheet (continued)

Georgia Performance Standards	Diagnostic Test	CRCT Practice Test	Test Preparation Workbook
M8N1.j Express and use numbers in scientific notation.	ITEM	ITEM	19–20
	19, 20	11, 12	
	CORRECT	CORRECT	
	___/2	___/2	
M8N1.k Use appropriate technologies to solve problems involving square roots, exponents, and scientific notation.	ITEM	ITEM	21–22
	21, 22	13, 14	
	CORRECT	CORRECT	
	___/2	___/2	
M8G1.a Investigate characteristics of parallel and perpendicular lines both algebraically and geometrically.	ITEM	ITEM	23–24
	23, 24	15	
	CORRECT	CORRECT	
	___/2	___/1	
M8G1.b Apply properties of angle pairs formed by parallel lines cut by a transversal.	ITEM	ITEM	25–26
	25, 26	16, 17	
	CORRECT	CORRECT	
	___/2	___/2	
M8G1.c Understand the properties of the ratio of segments of parallel lines cut by one or more transversals.	ITEM	ITEM	27–28
	27, 28	18	
	CORRECT	CORRECT	
	___/2	___/1	
M8G1.d Understand the meaning of congruence: that all corresponding angles are congruent and all corresponding sides are congruent.	ITEM	ITEM	29–30
	29, 30	19, 20	
	CORRECT	CORRECT	
	___/2	___/2	
M8G2.a Apply properties of right triangles, including the Pythagorean Theorem.	ITEM	ITEM	31–32
	31, 32	21, 22	
	CORRECT	CORRECT	
	___/2	___/2	
M8G2.b Recognize and interpret the Pythagorean Theorem as a statement about areas of squares on the sides of a right triangle.	ITEM	ITEM	33–34
	33, 34	23, 24	
	CORRECT	CORRECT	
	___/2	___/2	
M8A1.a Represent a given situation using algebraic expressions or equations in one variable.	ITEM	ITEM	35–36
	35, 36	25	
	CORRECT	CORRECT	
	___/2	___/1	

Georgia Performance Standards	Diagnostic Test		CRCT Practice Test		Test Preparation Workbook
M8A1.b Simplify and evaluate algebraic expressions.	ITEM		ITEM		37–38
	37, 38		26, 27		
	CORRECT		CORRECT		
	___/2		___/2		
M8A1.c Solve algebraic equations in one variable, including equations involving absolute values.	ITEM		ITEM		39–40
	39, 40		28		
	CORRECT		CORRECT		
	___/2		___/1		
M8A1.d Interpret solutions in problem contexts.	ITEM		ITEM		41–42
	41, 42		29		
	CORRECT		CORRECT		
	___/2		___/1		
M8A2.a Represent a given situation using an inequality in one variable.	ITEM		ITEM		43–44
	43, 44		30, 31		
	CORRECT		CORRECT		
	___/2		___/2		
M8A2.b Use the properties of inequality to solve inequalities.	ITEM		ITEM		45–46
	45, 46		32		
	CORRECT		CORRECT		
	___/2		___/1		
M8A2.c Graph the solution of an inequality on a number line.	ITEM		ITEM		47–48
	47, 48		33		
	CORRECT		CORRECT		
	___/2		___/1		
M8A2.d Interpret solutions in problem contexts.	ITEM		ITEM		49–50
	49, 50		34		
	CORRECT		CORRECT		
	___/2		___/1		
M8A3.a Recognize a relation as a correspondence between varying quantities.	ITEM		ITEM		51–52
	51, 52		35, 36		
	CORRECT		CORRECT		
	___/2		___/2		
M8A3.b Recognize a function as a correspondence between inputs and outputs where the output for each input must be unique.	ITEM		ITEM		53–54
	53, 54		37		
	CORRECT		CORRECT		
	___/2		___/1		

Grade 8 Georgia Diagnostic Scoring Sheet (continued)

Georgia Performance Standards	Diagnostic Test	CRCT Practice Test	Test Preparation Workbook
M8A3.c Distinguish between relations that are functions and those that are not functions.	ITEM 55, 56 CORRECT ___/2	ITEM 38 CORRECT ___/1	55–56
M8A3.d Recognize functions in a variety of representations and a variety of contexts.	ITEM 57, 58 CORRECT ___/2	ITEM 39, 40 CORRECT ___/2	57–58
M8A3.e Use tables to describe sequences recursively and with a formula in closed form.	ITEM 59, 60 CORRECT ___/2	ITEM 41, 42 CORRECT ___/2	59–60
M8A3.f Understand and recognize arithmetic sequences as linear functions with whole number input values.	ITEM 61, 62 CORRECT ___/2	ITEM 43, 44 CORRECT ___/2	61–62
M8A3.g Interpret the constant difference in an arithmetic sequence as the slope of the associated linear function.	ITEM 63, 64 CORRECT ___/2	ITEM 45 CORRECT ___/1	63–64
M8A3.h Identify relations and functions as linear or nonlinear.	ITEM 65, 66 CORRECT ___/2	ITEM 46 CORRECT ___/1	65–66
M8A3.i Translate among verbal, tabular, graphic, and algebraic representations of functions.	ITEM 67, 68 CORRECT ___/2	ITEM 47, 48 CORRECT ___/2	67–68
M8A4.a Interpret slope as a rate of change.	ITEM 69, 70 CORRECT ___/2	ITEM 49 CORRECT ___/1	69–70
M8A4.b Determine the meaning of the slope and y-intercept in a given situation.	ITEM 71, 72 CORRECT ___/2	ITEM 50, 51 CORRECT ___/2	71–72

Georgia Performance Standards	Diagnostic Test	CRCT Practice Test	Test Preparation Workbook
M8A4.c Graph equations of the form $y = mx + b$.	ITEM	ITEM	73–74
	73, 74	52	
	CORRECT	CORRECT	
	___/2	___/1	
M8A4.d Graph equations of the form $ax + by = c$.	ITEM	ITEM	75–76
	75, 76	53	
	CORRECT	CORRECT	
	___/2	___/1	
M8A4.e Determine the equation of a line given a graph, numerical information that defines the line, or a context involving a linear relationship.	ITEM	ITEM	77–78
	77, 78	54, 55	
	CORRECT	CORRECT	
	___/2	___/2	
M8A4.f Solve problems involving linear relationships.	ITEM	ITEM	79–80
	79, 80	56	
	CORRECT	CORRECT	
	___/2	___/1	
M8A5.a Given a problem context, write an appropriate system of linear equations.	ITEM	ITEM	81–82
	81, 82	57	
	CORRECT	CORRECT	
	___/2	___/1	
M8A5.b Solve systems of equations graphically and algebraically, using technology as appropriate.	ITEM	ITEM	83–84
	83, 84	58	
	CORRECT	CORRECT	
	___/2	___/1	
M8A5.c Interpret solutions in problem contexts.	ITEM	ITEM	85–86
	85, 86	59	
	CORRECT	CORRECT	
	___/2	___/1	
M8D1.a Demonstrate relationships among sets through use of Venn Diagrams.	ITEM	ITEM	87–90
	87, 88	60	
	CORRECT	CORRECT	
	___/2	___/1	
M8D1.b Determine subsets, complements, intersection, and union of sets.	ITEM	ITEM	91–92
	89, 90	61	
	CORRECT	CORRECT	
	___/2	___/1	

Grade 8 Georgia Diagnostic Scoring Sheet _(continued)_

Georgia Performance Standards	Diagnostic Test	CRCT Practice Test	Test Preparation Workbook
M8D1.c Use set notation to denote elements of a set.	ITEM 91, 92 CORRECT ___/2	ITEM 62 CORRECT ___/1	93–94
M8D2.a Use tree diagrams to find the number of outcomes.	ITEM 93, 94 CORRECT ___/2	ITEM 63 CORRECT ___/1	95–96
M8D2.b Apply addition and multiplication counting principles.	ITEM 95, 96 CORRECT ___/2	ITEM 64 CORRECT ___/1	97–98
M8D3.a Find the probability of simple, independent events.	ITEM 97, 98 CORRECT ___/2	ITEM 65, 66 CORRECT ___/2	99–100
M8D3.b Find the probability of compound, independent events.	ITEM 99, 100 CORRECT ___/2	ITEM 67 CORRECT ___/1	101–102
M8D4.a Gather data that can be modeled with a linear function.	ITEM 101, 102 CORRECT ___/2	ITEM 68 CORRECT ___/1	103–106
M8D4.b Estimate and determine a line of best fit from a scatter plot.	ITEM 103, 104 CORRECT ___/2	ITEM 69, 70 CORRECT ___/2	107–108